When "forgiveness"
   denies
      that there is anger,
  acts
      as if it never happened,
  smiles
      as though it never hurt,
  fakes
      as though it's all forgotten—

Don't offer it.
Don't trust it.
Don't depend on it.

It's not
   forgiveness
It's
   a magical fantasy.

CARING ENOUGH TO NOT FORGIVE

False Forgiveness

David Augsburger

HERALD PRESS
Scottdale, Pennsylvania
Kitchener, Ontario

Contents

Prologue

On the
One Hand

"Forgiveness," as it is frequently understood, is nothing one would give to a friend. It is neither blessed to give nor to receive.

On the one hand, only through the final form of love, forgiveness, is life together and community with each other truly possible.

On the other hand, forgiveness has its many counterfeits. Every virtue has its own shadow side where it is distorted into a vice, and not the least of these is forgiveness.

Forgiveness as it is frequently practiced is a process of denial, distortion, isolation, or undoing which leads to behaviors of avoidance, distancing, and spiritual alienation. Any stance of superiority, super-spirituality, or unilateral self-sacrifice reduces the possibility of real repentance and reconciliation.

Biblical agape is equal regard which refuses to

stand one-up over another or to live in denial, avoidance or distance. Thus it continues loving and living out the works of love as an invitation to the genuine mutuality of forgiveness. It sees the real focus of forgiving not in individualistic release from guilt and proof of goodness, but in interpersonal reconciliation, wholeness and life together in Christian community.

When "forgiveness"
puts you
one-up,
on top,
in a superior place,
as the benefactor,
the generous one,
the giver of freedom
and dignity—

Don't trust it,
don't give it,
don't accept it.

It's not
forgiveness;
It's sweet
saintly
revenge.

1 ■ Don't Forgive

When "Forgiveness" Puts You One-Up

"Forgive you? Of course not."

The man stiffened, confused, as his wife held him with her level gaze. He had just surfaced from the shame and guilt which had followed public exposure. "Will you forgive me," he had just asked, tentatively, doubtfully.

"No," she replied, but her face spoke acceptance, not rejection.

He did not hear the gentleness in her voice. He froze into painful silence, then regrets spilled out again. He had betrayed her trust, the trust of the whole community by becoming sexually intimate with two persons he was committed to help as a skilled counselor.

"No, I will not forgive you. I do not want the kind of relationship with you in which you are the offender and I the forgiver. I don't want you grateful and indebted to me for the rest of our lives. I want us to work through this until we both understand our parts in the problem, until we can accept each other."

"But I'm the one who hurt you, them, the community," he said.

"You did the active part. I did the passive part in helping create a relationship that was open to outside invitations. Let's work it out until we're back together."

Now he can see the caring, the respect, the determination in her eyes. She's wanting an equal relationship where mutual acceptance is genuine, and one-way-forgiveness cannot create it. Instead it would freeze a relationship in permanent inequality and injustice. Having seen such a bloodless solution to a marriage in trouble in her family of origin, she is not about to set herself up to repeat it in her own. So she says no to quick solutions that assign the fault to one party in a two-or-more-person problem.

Once Down, Always Down

When forgiveness puts you in a one-up position, care enough to not forgive.

One-up-forgiveness is an emotion which exists solely in connection with judgment and condemnation.

To say, "I forgive you," is to say, "I have examined, weighed, judged you and your behavior and found you sorely lacking in qualities that are worthy of my respect. I have these qualities at this point in time, but you do not. I humbly recognize my superior moral strength and your weakness, my consistent moral behavior and your inconsistency or immorality. I forgive you your trespasses. We will henceforth have a relationship based on the recognition of my benevolence in the hour of your neediness, my generosity in the face of your guilt. You will find some suitable way to be dutifully grateful from this day forward."

The forgiven person is aware, consciously or unconsciously, of being in a morally subordinate position. Permanently indebted, he or she must live out the repayment. This evokes resistance and resentment which clouds the relationship with contradictory emotions. To express the resentment or anger this evokes would make the forgiver look even more unworthy of the other's magnanimous "love." Thus it must be buried all the more deeply under strata of gratitude on gratitude. No one likes being that grateful, nor do they find that the obligations of "grateful obedience or compliance" offer any positive fulfillment to the relationship. Love does not flourish between unequals, and it does not grow when one is put down to meet the other's needs. Instead, once down, one is always down. To truly care, neither goes down, either affirms equality.

Once Indebted, Forever Indebted

"Yes, you forgave me readily, much too readily," she said, at last finding the courage to confront with thoughts that had burned in her for a long time.

"I told you about my love for Jim. You listened, you heard what I had done, you didn't ask for any details, and you said, OK, I forgive you. Let's forget it and go on, fine, that's what I wanted, I thought. But now I know that there was a hidden cost. I've been paying for it ever since.

"When I have any grievance against you, how can I share it? You go into your 'forgiving attitude' and I wind up the bad guy.

"When there's any real difference between us,

you're always the winner, and without really trying. How could I demand that things go my way when you are so understanding, so willing to overlook our disagreements?

"It's like I'm in the red, indebted for the rest of my life. If you could make just one real mistake, I'd feel human with you again."

To be plunged into the red, permanently, is intolerable for most persons, especially when the significant others nearby are obviously in the black and are not likely to let you escape it. And it is those in the black who are most likely to remind you of your place in the red, to not let you forget it.

Such forgiveness comes at too great a cost. It is no gift at all, it is earned and earned and earned. Once indebted, one is forever indebted.

To truly care, neither continues indebtedness, either moves to set both free from debts, and debtors.

Once Obligated, Always Obliged

"I was an orphaned refugee kid when World War II ended," Friedrich explains. "The childless couple who gave me a home until I left as a teenager were incredibly strict. Apparently I was in rags when they found me; I remember their giving me clean, unpatched, warm, used clothes. They burned my old ones in the kitchen stove as I watched. All but the shoes. At the last moment, father rescued them, and placed them on the mantel. They stayed there, I hear, until he died. They were only the battered uppers, laced with twine. The soles had long since worn away, and the bottoms were stuffed with cardboard each morning to protect the bare feet inside.

"I soon learned how useful they would be to him.

When I disappointed him in some way, he would walk to the mantel and pick up the shoes. When I resisted the strict control or complained about anything other kids were able to do and I was not allowed, he would look at the shoes. By the time I was a teenager, he didn't need to haul them down to remind me how much he and my mother had done for me, a glance was enough.

"When at 16 I finally protested being intimidated with worn out shoes, father looked at me as if I had struck him. 'I should think' he said stiffly, 'that you'd be grateful we never tried to make you feel grateful.'

"I'd have given anything as a boy to feel free of obligations, to give them my thanks as a gift, but it wasn't possible. I owed them everything except my life, and they had saved that, so by the time I was able to put my predicament into words, I no longer felt grateful at all."

Once in the Red, Always in the Red

When forgiveness is handed down from superior to inferior, from forgiver to forgivee, it places the forgiven in the red. To be in the red is to feel a burden of obligations, duties, demands, debits and general indebtedness weighing one down in an oppressive and depressive way. The feeling of being in an emotional deficit may be temporary or permanent, depending on what it does for either party or for both.

For the one on top, the rewards of generosity are immediate. "It is more blessed to give than to receive," the apostle Paul quotes Jesus, (Acts 20:35 *RSV*). The nearest parallel comment recorded in the Gospels is Jesus' reference to those givers who do their contributing in public places where their generosity will be admired. "They have their instant rewards" (see Matt.

6:1-5), He says in irony and accuracy.

To be a benefactor is an attractive experience to most persons. The rewards are multiple although mixed in character. To the giver:

- It offers a sense of service and helpfulness
- It gives opportunity for a self-sacrificial sense of "goodness"
- It can provide a release from one's guilt
- It provides a sense of superiority
- It allows one to be in control
- It confirms that the other—not the giver—is the one in need
- It opens an escape from facing one's own needs and hurts
- It obligates another to be grateful.

The benefits of receiving help are mixed as well. To the receiver:

- It offers escape from responsibility for a part of one's life
- It allows a return to dependency on another
- It requires the surrender of a part of one's control
- It affirms one's helpfulness, weakness, shame or guilt
- It is a recognition of an area of inferiority
- It indebts, obligates, turns gratitude into a duty.

Obviously, receiving appears less blessed, at first blush, than giving. When one is in the "indebted position" the immediate response for most is, "How can I ever repay you?" or, "I'll make it up to you some way, as soon as I can." The awareness of being "emotionally and relationally in the red" immediately pushes one toward regaining balance. Each person's beginning equilibrium is slightly different. Some are skewed toward needing to help, serve, rescue. Others are weighted toward the reverse with a need to submit, yield, cling or be dependent. While some tend to control, dominate or direct, others desire direction and domination. These biases can predispose a person to lean on others in a continuing one-down position, or to stand above others in a constant one-up stance.

"Now hold it right there, if there's any forgiving to be done around here, it will be done by me!" a one-up minister was overheard in a tense moment of conflict with an associate. One-up as a giver, he will press to stay "up" as a forgiver.

"I'm sorry, I blew it. Excuse me for living, I won't do it again," a one-down person says, reconfirming a chronic apologetic position. Once down, he's likely to stay down in a yielding, submitting style of relating to others. Nudged into the red by his own failure and driven further by the other's willingness to see him as inferior and indebted, he is not likely to surface into equal regard.

In true caring, obligations get obliterated, neither keeps the other in the red, either moves to affirm freedom and equality.

Once Inferior, Inevitably Inferior

Forgiveness refuses superiority. Forgiveness repudiates inferiority. Forgiveness occurs among people who perceive each other as equal, as equally worthful, as equally valued and valuable.

Much too much "forgiving," of course, accepts a person on the basis of his or her admitting inferior behavior, inferior feelings, and inferior worth. These self-negations are confirmed by the act of "forgiveness," so once inferior, inevitably inferior. Once induced to estimate worth by the painful failure, from now on "forgiveness" will keep him in his place, or hold her in her level.

Having failed, he will now be known by that failure.

Having fallen short in one experience, she will be short-changed according to that transaction. An act of lying identifies one as a lifetime liar. An act of adultery labels one as an adulterer forever (shades of *The Scarlet Letter*). Just as one successful act does not elevate one to the status of eternal success, or one brilliant thought does not certify one as first-rank genius on all thoughts. Just as a Nobel Prize in chemistry hardly guarantees that a person will have the last word in genetics, theology, or ethics, so a public exposure of failure in one area of life does not obliterate the insights, gifts, achievements, and contributions of all the rest.

In real caring, neither finds comfort, fulfillment or satisfaction in continuing any inequality. Either one will move toward mutual regard.

Redirect Such Forgiveness

Vertical forgiveness exchanges one sin against loving relationship for another. Where the original sin is an alienating offense against another which puts him or her in open pain, superior "forgiving" puts the offender down in a covert, hidden alienation. The second is the forgiver's subtle revenge. The put-down into long-term indebtedness can be like signing a lifetime mortgage on one's self-esteem, with the interest payable upon demand.

Whenever any element of superiority or any feelings of coming down on the other rise within you, refuse it. Redirect it. Reach out to the other, not down. Stand over against, not above. Stand with, not over. Stand equal in working through to forgiveness; otherwise we are trading one sinful position for another.

Sin is positional because it is a relational violation of another. We define positions by use of prepositions

**Generous benevolent
one-way forgiveness**

One-up

Dominate
Control
Direct
Help
Rescue
Serve

**Equal
Concern
for mutual
solutions** ←→ One-to-one
"We are forgiven" ←→ **Equal
Regard
for two-way
forgiveness**

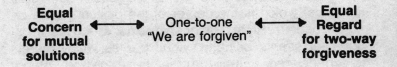

Submit
Yield
Depend
Cling

One-down

**Indebted "grateful"
one-way forgiveness**

FIGURE 1

(pre—meaning "before," how one thing is "positioned before" another) which express the relation of any noun, pronoun, or phrase to another element of a sentence. Personal relationships are defined prepositionally as the positions take form between individuals in their life situations or their living contracts.

I may choose to live *under you,* in yielding, submissive dependence, and from this position act as though you were my idol, my final good, my god. Or I may choose a superior position, standing *over you* in controlling, directing superiority, thus playing god. I may live *off of you* as a parasite, without you in withdrawal, *in spite of you* in individualism, or seek to live out my unlived life *in you* by absorbing and being absorbed.

All of these positions are sins against right relationships, which is the center of the biblical notion of righteousness. Right relationships exist where justice is done and seen to be done by both parties, where mercy is experienced mutually and jointly as persons stand *with each other* in steadfast love and where both walk in mutual respect before God. "Do justice, love mercy, walk humbly" is the view of the prophet Micah (see Micah 6:8) and of the Christ (see Matt. 5:1-12).

In caring—
- once down is not always down
- once indebted is not forever indebted
- once obligated is not always obligated
- once in the red is not always in the red
- once inferior is not inevitably inferior
- once at fault is not invariably at fault.

In caring
- equal regard, mutual respect, and joint movement toward right relationships spring up, nourish, flourish, and fill the emptiness of alienation with joyful reconciliation.

**Sin
is any choice
I make
or position
I take
to live—**

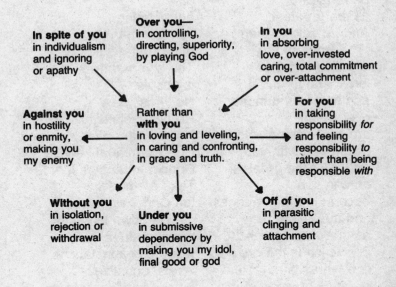

In spite of you
in individualism
and ignoring
or apathy

Over you—
in controlling,
directing, superiority,
by playing God

In you
in absorbing
love, over-invested
caring, total commitment
or over-attachment

Against you
in hostility
or enmity,
making you
my enemy

Rather than
with you
in loving and leveling,
in caring and confronting,
in grace and truth.

For you
in taking
responsibility *for*
and feeling
responsibility *to*
rather than being
responsible *with*

Without you
in isolation,
rejection or
withdrawal

Under you
in submissive
dependency by
making you my idol,
final good or god

Off of you
in parasitic
clinging and
attachment

FIGURE 2

Exploring the Biblical Basis

The temptation to stand over, above, in a superior (although humbly so) helping position springs eternal within the human heart. Jesus refused it, Jesus clearly rejected it as an appropriate stance for His followers.

Luke 22:24-27 (RSV)

A dispute also arose among them, which of them was to be regarded as the greatest. And he said to them, "The kings of the Gentiles exercise lordship over them; and those in authority over them are called benefactors. But not so with you; rather let the greatest among you become as the youngest, and the leader as one who serves. For which is the greater, one who sits at table, or one who serves? Is it not the one who sits at table? But I am among you as one who serves."

Comparison is the basis of pride. No one is proud of being great, but of being "greater than" or "the greatest of." The comparative is obsolete. No lordship *over*. No benevolence *over*. No standing *over*. Choose mutual service. Choose mutual respect. Take as model the Christ whose upside-down kingdom inverts values, reverses expectations levels, equalizes, erases superior/inferior distinctions and differences.

Philippians 2:5-11, (RSV)

Have this mind
among yourselves,
which you have in
Christ Jesus,
who, though he was
in the form of God,
did not count
equality with God
a thing to be grasped,
but emptied himself,
taking the form
of a servant,
being born in the
likeness of men.
And being found in
human form
he humbled himself
and became obedient
unto death,
even death on a cross.
Therefore God has
highly exalted him
and bestowed on him
the name which is
above every name, that
at the name of Jesus
every knee should bow,
in heaven and on earth
and under the earth, and
every tongue confess that
Jesus Christ is Lord, to
the glory of God the
Father.

Refusing to grasp
at equality with God
and superiority
over humanity,
He emptied Himself
of such claims.
He took a servant stance.
He stood "with"
and reached out.
His caring
does not insult;
His serving
does not belittle;
His giving
does not obligate.
His love
has no conditions.
His ministry is
a gift of respect—
even unto death.
God values
such loving.
(God *is* love.)
God honors
such caring.
(God is gracious.)
God prizes
such service.
(God comes as a Servant.)

It is in the nature of love that both subjects value each other equally, so that neither is seen as object. Love is a subject-subject relationship. Christ stood with others, truly with them in the identification of love, in incarnating love. He did not talk down, reach down, serve down. He stood *with*.

For Further Experience

Personally

1. Reflect on past experiences of forgiveness in which you felt one-down and were reaccepted by the other person from his or her superior position. How did you feel? Did the relationship ever recover mutuality? How long did it take?
2. Choose a recent experience of your forgiving. Draw a series of Xs on a paper to indicate your positions toward the other person during the series of experiences of (1) hurt, (2) anger, (3) sadness, (4) alienation, (5) confrontation, (6) negotiation, (7) trust restored, (8) love renewed, (9) forgiveness celebrated. How many positions did you occupy? Which are/were your favorite sins?

In Small Group

1. To experience the difference an emotional position of being "over" or "under" really makes, have two persons model this for the group. Stand one on a chair, pointing a finger of blame with one hand, offering a helping hand with the other. Have the other person kneel in one-down penance (being blamed) and earning (doing groveling). Each person identify the feelings aroused by each position. Then get off the chair and up from the floor and reach out as equals. Now share feelings. Note the difference

mutuality makes in trust, in love, in communication.
2. Complete any of the following lines which feel appropriate to gain each other's insight from forgiving/forgiven experiences.
  - I sometimes feel indebted to someone who forgives me, because . . .
  - I tend to feel inferior when another is very generous, benevolent and forgiving because . . .
  - I have been puzzled to discover that people I forgave completely are seldom grateful for the kindness, and I think . . .
  - I sometimes feel resentment when a person insists on accepting full responsibility for a misunderstanding between us, so I'd rather . . .
  - I am working at staying level with others in times of misunderstanding, and I'm doing it by . . .

When "forgiveness" is one
    way,
  calling one person to
    accept the difference,
    absorb the pain,
    adjust to injustice;
  don't rush to it,
  don't close the case with it.

It's not
  forgiveness,
It's
  loving submission.

2 ■ Don't Forgive

When "Forgiveness" Is One-Way

"I called home to see how my father was recovering from his heart attack only to discover that my mother was now in the hospital. At first they wouldn't tell me what was wrong; finally my sister let it out that she was in the psychiatric ward after taking an overdose. 'We didn't call you or tell you because you don't care about the family anymore, you're too good for us now.'

"I have never been cut so deeply in my life. I didn't sleep for two nights. My sister doesn't know I've been sending a fourth of my paycheck home each month to help cover the expenses for Dad's hospitalization. She doesn't know how often I call home, so what she said is not just unfair, it's really untrue.

"I prayed about it a lot, all night, in fact. I decided I'd never say another word about this to her. After all, she's been carrying quite a load at home. I'll just forgive her."

One-way forgiving seems generous, thoughtful, and self-sacrificial. It's generous, but not truly genuine. It's thoughtful but not thorough. It's self-sacrificial, but the sacrifice is seldom sufficient to restore the relationship.

One-Way Is the Way

When forgiveness is seen as a one-way, one-person affair, something indispensable is missing: *Reality.* Rarely can a familial, marital or work conflict be accurately defined as a one-person problem. Such is clearly the exception, not the rule. It takes two to have a continuing problem relationship. People don't have problems alone and people do not find healing and forgiveness alone.

Many acts of invasion, injustice and injury are inflicted on innocent parties. In such situations, forgiving may rightly be discussed as a one-person process, although even here the forgiveness is a partial, incomplete process which seldom concludes in a real reconciliation and the recovery of relationships. "Forgiveness" is the word most commonly used to describe such one-way acceptance of an offender, but it is partial forgiveness at best, more properly described as "love," since it is only the first step to forgiving, the primary step of restoring one's perceptions of love.

One-Way Is the Only Way

"If love is the one way to truly live, if love is the only way to freely live, then loving, living and forgiving all go together, right?"

Forgiveness and love commonly flow together in the questions people ask and the conclusions they draw. The two words are defined in identical ways, used as exchangeable terms, confused as one and the same. If the word *love* is substituted for most usages of the word *forgiveness*, nothing is lost in the meaning of the sentence. Love is a part of forgiveness, the first and basic part. Forgiveness begins when perceptions of love are restored and the other person is seen as valued, as worthful, as precious no matter what the wrongdoing. Then the real work of forgiving begins. Once love is restored then trust must be renegotiated until mutual trust is reexperienced by both, until right relationships have been restored or are now achieved.

When love is seen as the whole of forgiveness, then forgiving is viewed primarily as one-way. When an injury is received, a hurt inflicted, or trust betrayed, then the offended party—in one-way forgiveness—bears the loss, absorbs his or her own anger at the offense, and sets the other free. One-way is seen as the usual way. This is an act of love, a sacrifice of love, a gift of love. It is not forgiveness, it is only the preliminary step toward forgiving.

A case in point is *The Freedom of Forgiveness,* a popular best-seller on the nature of forgiveness. The writer, at that point in his life, saw forgiveness in a partial way. Typical of most writers on forgiving he illustrated, defined, applied it in a one-way style.

"The man who forgives pays a tremendous price— the price of the evil he forgives.

"If the state pardons a criminal, society bears the burden of the criminal's deed.

"If I break a priceless heirloom that you treasure and you forgive me, you bear the loss and I go free.

"Suppose I ruin your reputation. To forgive me, you must freely accept the consequences of my sin and let me go free!

"In forgiveness, you bear your own anger and wrath at the sin of another, voluntarily accepting responsibility for the hurt he has inflicted on you."[1]

A second writer, James Buswell, writes, "All forgiveness, human and divine, is in the very nature of the case vicarious, substitutional, and this is one of the most valuable views my mind has ever entertained. No one ever really forgives another, except he bears the penalty of the other's sin against him."[2]

When forgiveness is seen primarily as an act of one-side sacrifice, of one-way self-substitution, of one person absorbing the pain of another, then one-way is *the* way. There are times when sacrifice, acceptance, absorption are appropriate acts in forgiving, but they are the exception in times of extremity. Genuine forgiveness in ongoing relationships is not a unilateral action, but a mutual interaction. The basic model for genuine forgiveness is two-way, two-person, two movements toward reconciliation.

One-Way Is the Lonely Way

"I resented Jim for the way he worked against me at the factory. He gained nothing by undercutting me. I lost the promotion. I decided I'd never forgive him, not to my dying day. But I found I couldn't live that way. I was destroying myself with hate. It was no good, no good at all. I decided to live and let live, to forgive and forget."

One is a lonely number when a person is under stress or when relationships are distressed. To accept, absorb, adjust as an individual without interaction with the other party involved in the injury only increases the isolation and loneliness already involved in pain.

One alone can change his or her attitude toward another, can plan new behaviors in response to the

ONE WAY	**TWO WAY**
I am hurt,	There is pain
you are hurtful	between us
(I can forgive you)	(we can resolve it)
I am injured,	There are injuries
you have injured me	which separate us
(I can release you)	(we can remove them)
I am offended,	There are offenses
you are offensive	which alienate us
(I can accept you)	(we can forgive each other)

FIGURE 3

other, can put this into action toward the other, but until this is experienced with the other, forgiveness is frustrated.

In the family, when one sibling must make a silent adjustment to an alienated relationship with another, the interpersonal conflict gets absorbed and turned into an intrapersonal conflict. The hurt which existed between the two is internalized by one of the two. Loneliness results. The problem has just been moved, not removed.

In a marriage, when one partner chooses to make a private adjustment to a painful trauma between the two, it may reduce the tensions that separate them, but at a price. And as one person pays that price, loneliness increases, distance widens between them, and the marriage suffers a serious loss of openness and genuineness. Turning the pain of a relationship inward is no favor to the person or the relationship. The tensions are not being reduced, they are just getting recycled.

In working relationships, when one person opts to forgive in quiet acquiescence, the staff spirit may show improvement, but the progress is temporary. The trust level is blocked along with the obstructed communication. The loneliness of one human privately doing the work that rightfully belongs to two, of one person needing to secretly stifle the longing for open clear communication in order to maintain a surface of cooperation, slowly separates colleagues and turns them into polite strangers. The frustration is not being dissipated, it is displaced.

This stress on the importance of mutual forgiving flies in the face of most common understandings of what forgiveness is about. Most commonly it is taught as the one-way, one-up, one-for-all virtue. In fact, the superiority of one-way generosity, the "true spirituality" of unilateral altruism is so widely praised by preachers that real reconciliation has become the exception instead of the rule.

Individualism as a life-style has come to be understood as the real nature of mature living, individual love-styles are seen as the norm for resolving irritations; so individual solutions have replaced the joint solutions that create real community. The goal of forgiveness is reconciliation, not release. The task of forgiving is the reconstruction of the relationship, not pious retreat from real relating. One cannot do the real work of forgiving alone. One can restore his or her perception of love as an individual step. One can respond again to the other as a precious, valued and prized person. One can initiate conversation, invite real communication and do all that is within one person's power to create a genuine trusting-risking friendship. Yet it takes two to reconcile, two to realize that we are back in right relationships again. Trying to do all this in one-way action is a lonely way; one-way action leaves one wanting.

One-Way Is No Way

One-way is no way at all to work at authentically forgiven relationships. Most frequently it is a movement in the opposite direction.

▪ It is one-way to support denial of the real pain, of the actual strain on the relationship: "If you want to overcome the tension you have to learn to overlook it, to tolerate it, to ignore it and go on." Such a denial solution is not a resolution.

▪ It is one-way to support self-sufficient superiority, and so increase estrangement: "If you want to make things right you have to make the step yourself, take the whole step yourself." Such a self-confident solution stifles real resolution.

▪ It is one-way to stay in control, to manage the relationship to suit your own needs: "If you want it done right you have to do it yourself. You can't count on the other guy; you write it off as a loss and go on." Such managerial solution blocks the possibility of free resolution.

▪ It is one-way to make a self-righteous judgment against the other person as closed, incapable, insensitive, irresponsible or unconcerned: "If there's going to be any forgiveness between us it will have to be done by me; it would take forever if I were to wait for you." Such saintly solution is a false resolution.

▪ It is one-way to play safe by staying completely non-vulnerable, out of reach, impervious to the other's just criticisms or rightful demands: "How dare you criticize me after all I've forgiven you; how dare you be ungrateful after all I've put up with without complaint, after all I've forgotten." Such phoney "forgetting" solves nothing and resolves less.

▪ It is one-way to sin against community, to negate the equality of confessing our shared humanity, of standing with each other before God: "You just can't trust people with your real feelings, they'll only use them to get at you later on, to really hurt you. You've just got to be big about it, and rise above it all in forgiveness." Such "bigness of heart" is more often bigotry in the heart.

▪ It is the way to avoid making real contact with another, from covenanting in a genuine contract with another, from brothering and sistering each other: "Frankly you just have to learn to accept people for what they are. People are people."

Obviously, one-way solutions are appropriate to one-way personalities in one-way relationships, but

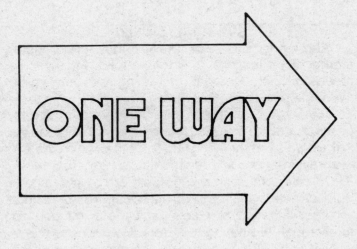

"If there's any forgiving to be done around here it will be done by me!"

"If there's any accepting to be offered by anyone it will have to be me!"

"If there's sacrifice to be made by anyone it will fall to me!"

FIGURE 4

they are powerless to create mutual, equal, reciprocal relationships of the love which is equal regard. For such relating, both give and take are indispensable; forgiving and fortaking blend in both persons.

Two-Way Is the Way

Forgiveness is a brother-brother, sister-sister, brother-sister process, a two-way mutual interaction of resolving differences and recreating relationships between persons of equal worth.

"Forgive us our debts as we forgive our debtors," Jesus taught His disciples to pray. It is the only condition in the Lord's Prayer (see Matt. 6:12). It is the only item in the prayer deserving a commentary (see Matt. 6:14,15). It is the only condition which is repeatedly underscored in Jesus' teaching (see Matt. 5:23; Matt. 18:15-18; Matt. 18:35). All these limit God's forgiveness to those who forgive their brothers and sisters. You will find this repeated in all of the crucial passages on forgiving (see Mark 11:25; Eph. 4:32; Col. 3:13).

To be forgiven, one must be forgiving.

To receive forgiveness, one must be willing to give forgiveness.

To refuse to forgive another is to refuse forgiveness for yourself. "Forgive as freely as God in Christ has forgiven you," is Paul's basic proposition on our need to give as voluntarily as God has given to us.

Two way acceptance is the way to forgiveness.

Mutuality is the heart of true forgiveness.

Reconciliation is the goal of genuine forgiveness.

Conciliation is the dialogue of persons seeking forgiveness.

Forgiveness is the mutual recognition that intentions are genuine and right relationships are restored or achieved.

Exploring the Biblical Basis

True forgiveness involves changes in both parties and in the community that surrounds them as well. When it is seen as one-way, reconciliation is rendered impossible. When the receiver also recognizes her opportunity to give, and the giver to receive, both move toward each other. This is the only issue in the Lord's Prayer which receives further commentary and even sharper application in Jesus' words which follow:

Matthew 6:12-15 (RSV)

And forgive us
our debts,
as we also have
forgiven our debtors;
and lead us not
into temptation
but deliver us
from evil.

For if you forgive
men their trespasses,
your heavenly Father
also will forgive you;
but if you do not forgive
men their trespasses,
neither will your Father
forgive your trespasses.

Ask only for that
which you are willing
to give to another.
Does this mean:
—as you receive, you
    must give?
—when you truly receive
    you gladly give?
—receiving and giving
    are the same thing,
    for forgiveness is
    one emotion of choosing
    faithfulness?
—forgiveness is two-way.
    The giver receives, the
    receiver gives, and to
    extend only one half
    invalidates both?

1. Is God then an eye-for-an-eye judge who keeps score on our practice and pays us back in kind?

2. Or is God an eternal bookkeeper who keeps ledgers on our behavior and holds us to our own decisions?

3. Or is God a loving forgiver who offers forgiveness but is not able to give it to the unforgiving heart, no matter how rich its piety?

4. Or does God view humans as responsible persons entrusted with the tasks of fidelity and God will not violate the integrity of their choices? So an unforgiving attitude puts one in an unforgiving state?

5. Or is the forgiveness of God given face, form, flesh and reality through my sister and brother, so that my refusal to forgive another, no matter how humble a person, is a flat refusal thrown into the face of God offered me in his or her human face?

6. Or what is your question from this passage? And what are your answers?

For Further Experience
Personally
1. Finish these lines on paper without editing or censoring your thoughts:
   a. Sometimes I'd like to just forgive and forget without having to talk about it so I . . .
   b. I kind of enjoy resenting for awhile because it lets me . . .
   c. I think it's better to overlook it when someone . . .
   d. I object to this definition of forgiveness as "two-way" because . . .
2. Now reread, reflect, reassess your responses. Make note of the things you thought of but did not write down. Welcome them as awarenesses which broaden your understanding of your own tendencies and preferences. Reaffirm at least two insights that

would have contributed to this chapter if you had written it.

In Small Group

1. Divide the group in two, assign one half to list five experiences of one-way wrongdoing requiring one-way forgiveness. The other group will list five experiences in which responsibility is shared and forgiveness must be mutually sought, reached, experienced. Now compare lists. Do you agree with the other team's judgments?

   Is there almost always some investment, some involvement even from an "innocent party?"

2. Now share around the circle in frank response to these:
   a. "Have I ever wronged another in a situation that was totally my fault?"
   b. "Have I ever been wronged in a way that was totally the other's doing?"
   c. "Is it hard for me to see how I sometimes ask for, contribute to, participate in, a conflict even when I know it is, to some degree, my problem too?

3. Offer each other gentle feedback on the above. Be tender with each other's blind spots. Is the mutual anxiety felt in this exchange of confrontations at all similar to the two-way involvement in any misunderstandings discussed in experience 2?

Notes

1. David Augsburger, *The Freedom of Forgiveness* (Chicago: Moody Press, 1970), p. 20.
2. J. O. Buswell, Jr., *A Systematic Theology of Christian Religion* (Grand Rapids: Zondervan Publishing House, 1962), vol. 2, p. 76.

When "forgiveness"
   distorts feelings by
   denying that there was
      hurt,
   disconnecting from
      feelings of pain
   squelching the emotions
      that rise,
   pretending that all is
      forgiven,
      forgotten
      forgone—

Don't trust it.
It's a mechanical trick.

3 ■ Don't Forgive

When "Forgiveness" Distorts Feelings

"The day he walked out on me, I knew it was over. Twenty-three years of tension, frustration, misunderstanding, anger, guilt and all that had come to a sudden halt.

"I packed up his clothes, pictures, and piles of junk. I put them in the back room and closed the door. Somewhere inside of me another door went shut too. That was the end. Case closed. I've not needed to go back and sort it out since then. A week later he showed up at the kitchen door, he wanted to come back. I told him it was too late. I had forgiven him all the misery he caused me the day I closed the storage room door. Just like that!

"Forgiveness is like turning a key in the lock. You never go back to look at it again. It's closed. Forever."

From her point of view, the marriage ended cleanly

in the closing of an emotional door. Tidy in housekeeping, she is also tidy with memory-keeping. Past, present and future, like three distinct rooms, can be entered or ignored at will. After 23 years of occupancy, the family room is now closed. Lock and key "forgiveness" seals away her past in a mausoleum of obsolete memories. Once laid to rest, it will not be revisited, reviewed or reclaimed for any possible learnings.

There are more accurate names for this variety of "forgiving." Clinically, it can be called isolation (a part of the self is isolated, sealed off, unavailable), denial (a wealth of feelings, thoughts, memories are denied and disowned) and repression (impulses, insights, and inner wisdom is repressed so it cannot come to awareness). If these words and definitions seem inappropriate or inaccurate as descriptions of distorted "forgiveness," consider these further examples of a variety of ways to evade forgiving by avoiding the other person.

Feelings? What Feelings?

"Sure, you gossiped about me to people in our congregation. You revived old stories from another time and place. I don't resent that at all. I can forgive you. I'm just sorry that you would stoop to such a level as to deliberately hurt someone with that kind of character assassination."

Denial is the family name for a whole clan of strategies for opting out of working through to forgiveness. Isolation, repression, reversal, undoing, and projection are the individual processes within the denial family. These denial mechanisms are ways of banishing intolerable memories, impulses, feelings and conflicts from consciousness. By use of one of these maneuvers, the person can disavow or disown these feelings or thoughts and in this way avoid acknowledging their painful nature.

Denial—"I saw nothing, heard nothing, felt nothing, said nothing, did nothing"—is the simplest and most direct form of avoiding real contact with another. By revising and rewriting the past to suit my present wishes I can avoid the threat of facing the realities of life.

A woman, accused of having stolen a valuable vase and breaking it in her haste to conceal the item, said to the people confronting her, "You will have to forgive me since I didn't take the vase to begin with. I'm not responsible for breaking it because it was chipped when I took it; and besides, I returned it in perfect condition."

In strained relationships, denial really comes into its colorful best. Relationships are at least two-person systems, so the possibilities of refusing responsibility and passing it back and forth are virtually endless. But the strategies used can be wonderfully subtle, often beyond the recognition of the person employing them.

Memory? What Memory?

"That's the way the cookie crumbles," Mike said, shrugging his shoulders coolly. "I'm sure Sandy will be able to overlook it all and forgive me, but the company won't. They'll be pressing charges."

Two hundred thousand dollars are missing from accounts. Mike is clearly the one responsible. The news is breaking in the media. His career is over. He will answer for it in court in the future. But at the moment, he has no feeling about it at all. The painful association between a thought—"I'm to be tried for embezzlement and I've no defense"—and its emotional counterpart is disconnected. Event and feeling are not linked. By detaching the feelings—shame, guilt, regret, an impulse to confess, repay, make restitution—from the event in question, he protects himself from overwhelming anxiety. And toward Sandy, his wife, he feels no shame, embarrassment or regrets for the pain this is causing her, assumes her "forgiveness."

Is this forgiveness? If so, it's a temporary solution. Isolation of emotion from actual experiences results in areas of deadness in the self, in a frozenness of feeling responses, and in the later return of unresolved tensions, fears, frustrations and resentments.

"Forget it, it didn't matter at all, it was nothing," I once said to a man who wanted to work through a past difficulty with me. On later reflection I discovered I had some feelings about his stiff words that I had closed off somewhere inside myself. "Why feel hurt about his insensitivity, he wasn't that important to me," I had decided deep within. Unfair. Untrue. And his coming back to initiate reconciliation had punched a hole in the wall of my internal isolation process; so finally recognizing the reality within, I could call him back. "I'm discovering I do have some feelings after all, let's talk."

Isolation (isolating feelings from thoughts) is a process that is learned early in childhood and then relearned in each experience of detaching awareness of an event from its emotional impact. It is terrifying for a child to be angry at the parent, because the parent is also needed so much. So the feeling gets separated and sealed off from the thought. It is bad to hate one's little sister who is taking away all the attention of people, so the resentment gets walled off from the recognition that one has been replaced.

So lock and key forgiveness fits nicely into this pattern. The hurt, anger, resentment and repayment needs are shut from awareness and absorbed by the body or go into an emotional slush fund. Among good people this is often given religious labels and a spiritual explanation.

"I've no right to be angry about it, no matter how much it hurts. God loves you and I must too. I forgive you for the bitter—I mean better—days to come."

"I pray for the grace to accept what comes in life. Sure, there are difficult times, but that doesn't matter. I don't let them affect my feelings. That's just the way things are."

Quarantining the negative feelings is no guarantee that they will not return to haunt future relationships. In fact, the reverse is most often true. Out of the slush funds of our unfinished feelings come old dated emotions to filter our new learnings and infiltrate our present feelings. Forgiveness is not isolating; it is integrating.

Angry? Who's Angry?

"When Al lost his temper in our group meeting last night and blamed me for causing him to lose his job and for turning others against him, I felt suddenly and totally calm. I just sat there in real concern for him. He didn't make me angry at all. He can say all the vicious underhanded demeaning things he wants to, I forgive him."

What is really happening for the speaker of these words? Read them again and put yourself in the speaker's place. Can you feel the double-tongued emotions coming out in two directions? Loving concern and at the same time cutting labels for the other person.

So frequently in conflict an inner mechanism provides an instantaneous release from tension. The negative feelings that would normally well to the surface are pressed down and not felt at all. When this response is instant and automatic, we say the responses were repressed. The repressing person is not consciously suppressing the feelings; he or she is not aware that it is happening at all. When attention is turned inward the negative feelings are nowhere to be seen. A screen of denial drops to hide them from view, and the only sign that they are lurking unsuspected behind all the positive words is the telltale hostility that comes out in tone of voice and in the judgmental attitude, words and innuendos between the lines. Read the opening statement again and note how the speaker was able to label Al's actions as "vicious underhanded demeaning" while also expressing "forgiveness." Something nasty is being repressed here, and it is even more so because it is hidden under the guise of loving and forgiving.

This simple involuntary process excludes one's undesirable thoughts and feelings from consciousness, but not without a price. It requires energy to keep such counter-energies in check and in concealment even from oneself.

To visualize this process, imagine a person sitting in a giant hot tub with all his or her repressed thoughts and feelings bobbing like corks in the water around. To repress them requires that they be held out of sight beneath the surface, but soon the person does not have enough hands. "Here, have a ham sandwich," another may offer, but the person hasn't a free hand. "Want to play catch?" someone cries. "Sure," the person says, "but I'm too busy."

Freedom comes as one can let the corks bob up one at a time, look at them, own them, decide what is best to do with them; discard those that are out of date, and deal with those that still have meaning. When both hands are free, the past is owned, used, accepted for what it is, and woven into present meaningful friendships. At last, out of the tub and on dry land, one can run, leap and dance again.

Any forgiveness which is won by repressing one's feelings and responding according to external authority will not result in reconciliation of both persons as whole persons. Forgiveness happens as past resentments are owned, not disowned; are recognized, not repressed; are released, not retained; and are woven into new bonding relationships with others.

I'm Not Upset, I'm Only Concerned

"You're angry at me, are you not?"

"No, I feel no anger. I'm only concerned."

Instead of anger, the emotion which was communicated to the questioner, the person is aware only of concern. This reversal of emotion is the constant companion of the forgiving experience; in fact it mimics forgiveness. In this reversal, the individual represses the negative emotions which are undesirable impulses and assumes a diametrically opposite conscious attitude. So a hostile person may display a facade of exaggerated amiability; a rebellious child may become scrupulously polite and gracious; a fragile person may act insensitive and demanding; a fearful person may come on authoritarian; a socially insecure woman may put out a blasé and worldly-wise manner. All this serves to help keep the negative energies under constant check.

In resolving a conflict, the temptation to go with such a reversal is great because the payoff is immediate for persons who are afraid of their own negative feelings. For example, I can repress my resentful side, which wants to put you down in anger, by expressing my super-helpful side, which gladly puts you down by showing my ability in the face of your present inability; my moment of adequacy in the presence of your momentary inadequacy. Such reversal is a means to meeting hidden needs for many people. A person who crusades in condemnation of public immorality may devote great amounts of spare time to "investigating" pornographic literature, houses of questionable repute, or censoring movies; at the same time this large investment of effort can gratify his own unrecognized lascivious desires even while he is consciously decrying the shameful state of public morality.

What's Past Is Past. Or Is It?

All of these strategies are ways of refusing to come to terms with one's past and its impact on present relationships.

By denying that what was, was and what is, is, I can stop time for myself and create a world that is less painful, less vulnerable, less threatening.

"I couldn't understand that the promotion had gone to Jim. He was less experienced, less qualified, and not related to anybody in the administrative committee. Then I overheard a conversation which filled in the missing piece. I was waiting in the outer office to file a report, the door to the personnel director's office was ajar, and I heard him dictating letters:

'Thank you for your frank reply to our reference form. Your information on our employee came as a complete surprise . . .'

"I listened, stunned by the discovery that I had been blackballed by the reference I'd trusted most. Why would Alex have done me in? We've known each other

Repress the feeling

"Of course I forgive you; it was nothing anyway."

Isolate the feeling

"You win some, you lose some, forget it. It's OK."

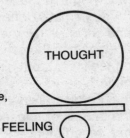

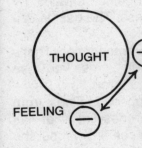

Reverse the feeling

"I'm not angry, no matter how badly you cut me down, I'm just concerned about you."

Deny the feeling
"Feelings? I don't have any feelings about what happened; let's forget it and go on."

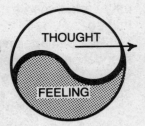

Integrate thought and feeling
"I do care about you; I also feel both sad and angry about what has happened between us. Let's work it through."

FIGURE 5

since college. I'd have trusted him with my prize '24 Ford. How could I even accept the fact that he had done it? How could I ever accept or forgive him again?"

Which of the available options will Jim choose in resolving this triangle?

1. "What's done is done. The job is gone. I'll adjust and get on with my work. As far as Alex is concerned, I'll not give him the satisfaction of being openly angry. I've no feelings about him at all. He can live his life. I'll live mine."

"Forgiveness" through denial of real feelings offers the benefit of release from the threat of one's own anger, resentment and awareness of being betrayed, by simply cutting them out of awareness. The past is dismissed.

2. "So Alex gave me a bad recommendation. That's the way the ball bounces. You win some, you lose some. That's that. There's nothing more to say."

"Forgiveness" through isolation of feelings from facts offers the advantage of awareness of what has happened and its impact upon the self but without the usual attachments of painful emotions. The past is detached.

3. "I can't believe that Alex gave me a bad recommendation. He must have reasons that I don't understand. I can forgive him for that; I'm just concerned about him and others who may be mistreated as I was."

"Forgiveness" through repression of real feelings and the expression of the reverse emotion offers escape from more explosive feelings in exchange for the more acceptable response. The past is distorted.

The past may be dismissed, but it will not disappear. One can detach from the past but it does not leave the memory, and distorting the past offers no lasting resolution to a conflict.

Exploring the Biblical Basis

Clear, open, genuine response to others in feeling, emoting and relating is modeled throughout the New Testament as "speaking the truth in love" as Paul describes it in Ephesians 4:15. To observe his own candid and focused expression of direct feelings and emotions, review the intense letter to the Galatians to see how this occurs in powerful yet gentle ways.

Emotion Expressed	Reference	Your Notes
astonishment	1:6	
outrage	1:8	
hostility (accursed!)	1:8,9	
defensiveness	1:10	
candid self-disclosing	1:11-24	
assertiveness	2:5	
sarcasm	2:6	
concern/compassion	2:10	
confrontation/accusation	2:11-21	
confrontation/concern	3:1-5	
disappointment	4:11	
affection/gratitude	4:12-15	
open honesty	4:16	
anger	4:17,18	
deep caring/compassion	4:19	
perplexed/frustrated	4:20	
confrontation	5:7	
confidence	5:8	
rejection/criticism	5:8	
violent (or sarcastic) anger	5:12	
love	5:13,14	
courage	6:9	
service/caring	6:10	
humility	6:14	
assertiveness	6:17	

1. Note how immediate and direct Paul is in expressing his feelings.

2. Note how unapologetic he is for all the negative emotions he is expressing. Fifteen out of 25 emotions in the above list are critical, hostile, even violent (or is it sarcastic) anger.

3. Note how his feelings are focused on restoring open communication, 4:16, true freedom in community, 5:1,13,25.

4. Note carefully his summary of destructive emotions and actions, 5:15-21, and of the constructive emotions and actions which are the evidences of the Spirit, 5:22-25.

5. Reflect on how direct (undistorted) Paul's feelings are, how genuine (undenied) his response is.

For Further Experience

Personally

1. Finish the line—"I sometimes repress the feeling of _____ for days before I am aware of my negative emotions. (Finish this several times to recognize multiple feelings.)

2. Finish the line—"I sometimes isolate feelings of _____ so that I am (circle one) numb / uninvolved / aloof / neutral / distant / bored / in a situation of tension or misunderstanding. (Reflect on this to welcome inner feelings to be more available in times of conflict.)

3. Plan times of reflection. "After a puzzling time of confusing feelings, I will take time to sort out what is going on inside me so that the delay between occurrence and recognition is shortened." (Make a concrete plan for a 30-day period for reviewing your

feelings and choosing appropriate ways of expressing or accepting and dismissing them.)

In Small Group

1. Choose a recent conflict situation from one group member's experience, or from the recent group process, and roleplay the scene four different ways.
   a. Everyone isolate feelings by choking them off and being very very neutral, intellectual, computer-like without the intrusion of "emotional baggage or garbage."
   b. Reverse the feelings by saying positive things instead of negative, socially accepted feelings instead of real ones, nice smiles instead of genuine honesty, super-helpfulness instead of confrontation. . . .
   c. Deny the feelings. After each comment about the conflict, add a denial—"of course it doesn't matter to me," "I couldn't care less," "I have no feelings about that at all," etc.
   d. Now integrate feeling and thought. Share ideas and feelings side by side in each sentence. "I think and I feel . . ."
2. Discuss the above exercise by applying it to past experiences of giving or receiving forgiveness. Better yet, apply it to a recent or present tension felt with someone in the group. Integrate thought and feeling as you resolve it now. Or rehearse a dialogue you need to have with someone else (without giving name, sex and any other clues to avoid gossiping). Decide when you will go to the other and pledge accountability with the group to report back (still maintaining confidentiality).

When "forgiveness"
  denies
    that there is anger,
  acts
    as if it never happened,
  smiles
    as though it never hurt,
  fakes
    as though it's all
    forgotten—

Don't offer it.
Don't trust it.
Don't depend on it.

It's not
  forgiveness
It's
  a magical fantasy.

4 ■ Don't Forgive

When "Forgiveness" Denies Anger

"I'm not angry, as God knows my heart, I'm only concerned that Jim get his life straightened out. Sure, he's ruining my daughter's life with his fooling around and I worry about what his example will do to little Jimmy. But I forgive him. What else is there for a Christian to do?"

Is there no anger in this father's heart? Yes, yes there is, despite his conscious denials. Later he will be free to own it and deal with it more honestly.

Is there no place for anger in a compassionate person's life? Yes, yes there is, not in spite of the love felt for the other but because of, and in expression of, the love for another.

Is there no other choice but to forgive in a painful situation like this? Yes, yes there are other choices, other steps that will lead to true forgiveness rather than drawing a blanket of conscientious denial over the whole situation. This father feels tension tearing at him, stretching his integrity to the breaking point.

"I feel all torn apart at times. I must forgive. If we do not forgive others their trespasses, neither will ours be forgiven; yet it seems to me that I have some things to say to him, some demands to make. Right is still right whether I forgive him or not, and what he is doing is not right. How do I live with that? If forgiving does not call for some reconstruction, what then? Is there nothing more to say?"

Anger—Constructive or Destructive?

Anger has many faces. And anger faces in two contrasting directions. One direction is toward destructive annihilation of the offender or the offense. The other is toward constructive affirmation of both self and other in rebuilding the offensive relationship and restoring the offending person.

Destructive anger turns its face away, rejecting the other and refusing open relating. It tears away from the loving contact to sever the trusting connection. Such malignant aggression can either fester and ferment within the person or explode and ventilate on the other. By itself, it is powerless to effect any creative change because it is destructive in its essential core.

Constructive anger turns toward the other person, moving the other to restore contact, raging against the walls of misunderstanding or the treadmills of repetitious misbehavior that divide and alienate us. Such benign aggression can break down the intervening barriers and break through the confusion that separates persons. Its intention and its actions are essentially

CONSTRUCTIVE ANGER	DESTRUCTIVE ANGER
Affirmation of both parties in rebuilding the offended relationship and restoring the offender.	Annihilation of both the offender and the offense.
Turns toward—to break through the wall. Moves toward—to restore contact.	Turns away—to create distance. Tears away—to sever contact.
In the love-hate balance, hate is directed toward the wall of misunderstanding that separates/alienates us. Love is affirmed toward the other person in the situation.	In the love-hate balance, hate is directed toward the person who is blamed for the alienation. Love is attached to the lost relationship, security or thing.

FIGURE 6

creative, even though it may be breaking up old patterns of acting and being in recreating life together.

Love and unlove are always mixed. In affirming the deep commitment of love toward another, one is also asserting his or her apposition to all that stands against that love. So love is almost inevitably mixed with hate. In a situation of perceived wrongdoing, the love-hate balance may tip constructively or toward destruction. In destructive anger, the balance of love and hate tips toward the negative side. Hate is directed toward the offending person, the blame for the alienation is laid at that person's doorstep, and what love remains is attached to the lost relationship, the lost security, or the things lost in the difficult situation. In constructive anger, the hate is directed toward the wall of misunderstanding that separates and estranges us. Love is recognized in the deep concern that energizes the anger and in the investment in being heard, understood and respected.

Angry Love or Loving Anger

Love that pretends to be total, with no recognition of the admixture of its opposite emotions, tends to drive the anger into unawareness and recycle it into other emotions. Angry love is loving, accepting, forgiving on the surface but frustrated within. Since the concern for the other often emerges from deep commitments to care for people, acknowledging negative feelings is not easy.

Love that intends perfection, with no room for the negative feelings, forces one to repress emotional frustrations as well as rational demands. Both are important parts of the person, both are needed in working through to real reconciliation. Unowned anger contaminates love, unrecognized resentment blocks the free expres-

**NO
CONDITIONS
FOR
LOVING** = **MANY
CONDITIONS
FOR
LIVING**

IN
FORGIVING,
LOVE IS RESTORED
(NO CONDITIONS
FOR LOVING)
AND
TRUST IS ACHIEVED
(THE CONDITIONS FOR
LIVING REACH MUTUALLY
SATISFACTORY SOLUTIONS).

FIGURE 7

sion of acceptance and affection. What is offered instead is angry love.

Loving anger accepts and expresses both the love and the anger. Both are caring, concerned, bonding emotions which can be used constructively or destructively. Each is to be prized. Each must be used wisely. Anger is traditionally suspect. Love is habitually admired. But both can be equally evil. Persecution is most thorough when the persecutor believes he is doing you a service. Beware and be wary when anyone says, "I'm only doing this for your own good."

Love and anger expressed in ways that create trust, create respect, create mutuality, create an equal relationship, can be a gift. The anger must be channeled to be useful in building relationship. The love must be the equal regard which values self and other in equivalent ways to be liberating and connecting.

In forgiving, both love and anger meet. Love accepts the other without conditions. (There can be no conditions for loving.) Anger presses for justice in relationships with clear conditions. (There are many conditions for living.)

Just and Unjust Demands

Inside all my feelings of anger, there are demands. Often conflicting demands. At times there are many-layered demands.

There are just demands. When I am not equally heard, I feel the demand for equal justice in communication. When I am not seen as trustworthy and I have acted in good faith, I feel the demand for equal trust. When I am not valued as a person, I feel the demand for equal regard. These are demands grounded in the justice of our equal created worth.

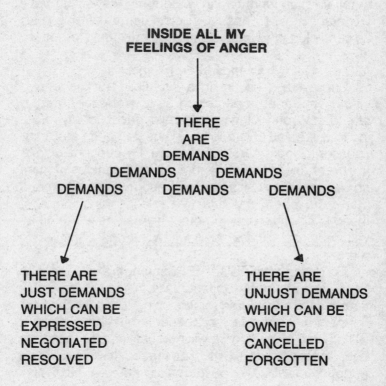

**INSIDE ALL MY
FEELINGS OF ANGER**

THERE
ARE
DEMANDS
DEMANDS   DEMANDS
DEMANDS   DEMANDS   DEMANDS

THERE ARE
JUST DEMANDS
WHICH CAN BE
EXPRESSED
NEGOTIATED
RESOLVED

THERE ARE
UNJUST DEMANDS
WHICH CAN BE
OWNED
CANCELLED
FORGOTTEN

FIGURE 8

And there are unjust demands. I may demand that you think as I think, feel as I feel, act as I act. I may demand that you know what I wish without my needing to tell you, do what I wish without my respecting your voluntary choice. These are unjust demands which can be cancelled, and then, as finished business, forgotten.

Demands in Forgiveness

Forgiveness occurs in a situation of experienced injury. The other is perceived as a wrongdoer, as the offender. Wrongdoing is not a valid reason for my refusing to value and love another. Thus demands as conditions for loving are not appropriate. Perceptions of love are prerequisite to forgiveness. No negotiations of trust, no willingness to risk again, no freedom to venture once more into open and effective relationships, none of these is possible until the other is seen as worthful, as valuable, as a friend and fellow human being once more.

Forgiving takes place as demands are dealt with honestly, forthrightly, and mutually. There are inevitably demands in any injured relationship. "It should not have happened. It should be changed. It must be undone. It will have to be paid for. It will hurt until someone suffers equally because of it. It must be erased. It will have to be forgotten. It will never be forgotten, etc., etc., etc." All of these demands are useless, they are powerless. There is no way that they can be performed, no way they can be seduced or coerced out of another without violating both.

In forgiving, one gives up the right to demand the impossible demand. One quits dreaming the impossible dream of forcing another to undo the past or promise the future in ironclad guarantees. One stops fighting the unwinnable battle of forcing the other to grovel, grieve or give some satisfaction. One drops all hopes of exacting repayment, atonement, expiation, or some subtle form of gratification. All this is still at the beginning point of forgiving, it is the starting line. But no real forgiving will happen until unjust demands are cancelled.

When anger is denied these demands go unowned, unfaced, unreleased. When anger is repressed these demands get recycled, and they reappear in more acceptable terms, often in saintly garb. Then the negotiation of the just demands, which can lead to mutual repentance, gets contaminated by the unjust, the impossible, the covertly revengeful. And the person acting out of hidden and unrecognized anger is not at all or only fleetingly aware of what is happening.

When anger is owned and clarified the unjust demands are dropped, often with a sense of humor, often with a release of laughter. To be able to chuckle at the instant swelling of god-like pretentions which rise in response to rage is to let go of them with gladness.

Then the just demands that continue can be expressed, negotiated, and mutual solutions sought.

Reflect again on Christ's modeling of clear and focused anger near the opening of His ministry. (See Mark 3:1-6.)

He entered the synagogue on the Sabbath, saw the hope for healing in the eyes of the man with a paralyzed hand, saw the calloused indifference and critical coldness on the faces of the waiting, watching Pharisees.

Jesus looked at them with anger. Then He expressed His demands. "Is it right to do good or to do evil on the Sabbath, to save life or to kill?" He asked. Then He acted in love.

Having clarified His anger and His concern for justice in direct address, He had opened the way for clear understanding between Himself and others. It was not accepted. It was not successful in achieving reconciliation. He respected their right to refuse Him.

Don't forgive easily, quickly, superficially without reflecting on your demands, cancelling the unjust ones and working through what remains. It is the way to real repentance and full forgiveness.

Exploring the Biblical Basis

Anger may be internalized and converted into bodily symptoms or diverted into distorted relationships. Or it may be owned, expressed responsibly and resolved creatively. Note the contrast between the two parallel passages in which Paul quotes but corrects David (Ps. 4; Eph. 4).

Psalm 4:
David's Strategy

How long will you love
vain words, and seek
after lies?
But know that the Lord
has set apart the
godly for himself;
the Lord hears when
I call to him.
Be angry, but sin not;
commune with your
own hearts
on your beds,
and be silent.
Offer right sacrifices
and put your
trust in the Lord.

Ephesians 4:
Paul's Counsel

Therefore putting away
falsehood,
let everyone speak the
truth with his
neighbor,
for we are members
one of another.

Be angry but do not sin;
do not let the sun go
down on your anger,
and give no opportunity
to the devil.

. . . .

In peace I will both lie down and sleep; for thou alone, O Lord, makest me dwell in safety. (vv. 2-8, *RSV*)

. . . .

Let all bitterness and wrath and anger and clamor and slander be put away from you, with all malice, and be kind to one another, tenderhearted forgiving one another, as God in Christ forgave you. (vv. 25-32, *RSV*)

Compare and contrast the setting, counsel and results of these two passages:

The Setting

David is speaking of a context of angry wrongdoing, dishonest ventilation and vilification. He contrasts this with the godly community which has been set apart by God to trust in the Lord in prayer, confidence, and right religious practice of religious ritual in worship (vv. 2,3,5)

Paul is speaking of a context of angry, hard, callous behavior, motivated by deceitful desires (vv. 17-23). He contrasts this with the new nature (v. 23), and the new community (v. 25) in which open honesty is possible.

The Counsel

David recommends silence, internalization, postponement, sleeping on the problem, working

Paul teaches open truth-speaking in clear negotiation with the neighbor, for we are it out in private piety.

David's anger returns again and again. Read Psalm 109 to see how he expresses bitterness, wrath, brooding anger, clamor, slander and malice on his bed.

members of the Body of Christ (vv. 25,26,30; 5:1,2).

Paul sees this open confession delivering us from bitterness, brooding wrath and rage, and other forms of harbored hostility.

The Results

For David, uncontrollable rage, murder, adultery, conspiring evil, break out impulsively in himself and in his children.

And his bed is miserable (read Ps. 6:6-8).

For Paul, clear negotiation of differences occurs with love and truth clearly expressed (Eph. 4:15; Gal. 2:11-21) in a community of trust (Eph. 5:1,2).

For an effective model of clear expression of anger, modeling of clarification of demands and forthright actions of concern, read again Mark 3:1-6. Note how open, genuine, focused and principle-oriented Jesus is in confronting closed condemning opponents who have cut off feeling. His clearly defined demands for true justice and mercy are expressed in both word and deed.

For Further Experience
Personally
1. To reflect on your own management of anger feelings, finish the lines (preferably on paper without

editing, censoring, polishing to suit your "ideal image").

I become angry when . . .

I get most irritated at . . .

I make me angry by demanding . . .

I resent . . .

2. To explore your demands, make two columns, one headed "just demands" and the other "unjust demands." Now list the demands inside the anger feelings which you have described in exercise 1. Plan ways to express just demands more effectively and constructively. Decide again to recognize, own and cancel the unjust demands in a clear act of will, humor, and choosing of freedom.

In Small Group

1. Use the unfinished lines from the personal column just preceding to invite all members of the group to self-disclose their ways of experiencing and expressing anger. Then go on to explore just and unjust demands on the most significant anger feeling each person expresses.
2. Turn to the page outlining constructive and destructive anger in this chapter. Have two volunteers model or roleplay these alternatives. Discuss until the distinction is clear and each person has been invited to share—if they choose—an example of one or both from their own life.
3. Each affirm one further goal in more useful management of anger feelings in working toward true forgiveness.

When "forgiveness"
    ends open relationships,
    leaves people cautious,
    twice shy,
    safely concealed,
    afraid to risk free
    open spontaneous
    living,
don't forgive.

It's not
    forgiveness.
It's
    private alienation.
It's
    individual estrangement.

5 ■ Don't Forgive

When "Forgiveness" Ends Open Relationship

"I have forgiven him. I do not fool myself that our relationship will ever be what it once was. Something that once united us in friendship is now destroyed."

A confidence was broken, private information was shared publicly, trust was violated. Now forgiveness has been affirmed but not truly felt. It has been put in words but not in deed. Having been put into words it is less likely to be put into action.

If I say I have forgiven another, I have given my word that the situation is complete, finished, closed. But if trust has not yet been negotiated and open relationships are not yet restored, our communication is blocked, understanding is frustrated, full acceptance is postponed.

"I can work with him without feelings but I will not risk

sharing anything personal in the future. 'Fooled me once, shame on you; fooled me twice, shame on me' we used to say, and that's the way it is. I trusted him then. He betrayed it. I'll not put him or me in that place again."

This is not forgiveness no matter what words are used. It *is* love, since respect has been reaffirmed, but the real work of forgiving has not yet begun.

Now the negotiations of trust must start; and unfortunately the two are no longer in conversation on the issue. Trust testing is seldom resumed after forgiveness has been affirmed.

Release Is the Goal

Forgiveness is release, release from a whole spectrum of negative emotions like fear, anger, suspicion, loneliness, alienation, mistrust. When the fear is disruptive, when the anger is destructive, when the suspicion estranges, when the loneliness depresses, then release can be healing.

But "release" can also be a way to flee real relationship. Where there is fear of working through the differences, fear of real confrontation, fear of what one may need to face in honest communication, then "forgiveness" can be a release from the threat of making peace.

Where there is anger that arises out of clear, fair and just demands that deserve clarification and negotiation, then release through "forgiveness" impoverishes both, and the moment of growth is lost.

Where there is suspicion that is creating escalating mistrust, then reporting and working through the loss of faith can be the best and perhaps the only way to achieve a new and lasting trust, and "forgiveness" will release that drive and the opportunity for keeping faith with each other is forfeited.

Where there is loneliness that signals the presence of distance between people, that indicates intimacy is betrayed, the only way to deal with that loneliness is not through finding a way out of the alienation in "forgiveness," but finding a way through in genuine encounter, or the moment of meeting is lost.

"Forgiveness" lets the alienated person off the hook, so that he can evade working through differences to real reconciliation.

"Forgiveness" is flight from the creative tensions that need to be resolved in genuine brotherly-sisterly address which leads to full reconciliation.

Reconciliation Is the Goal

"Forgiveness is necessary, reconciliation is optional," is the basic assumption underlying much teaching, thinking, writing, and counseling on the goal of forgiving.

One must forgive or he will not be forgiven. If one does not forgive her sister or brother, she will not be forgiven of God who forgives us our debts as we forgive our debtors. If I refuse to forgive another, the resentment, the brooding over retaliation, the desire for repayment can poison my own spirit. Forgiveness can set both self and other free.

Overhearing several friends denouncing their Civil War enemies, Abraham Lincoln is reported to have said, "Insane as it may seem, I hold malice toward none of them. I have neither the time nor the energy in this life to hold that kind of resentment."

Unfortunately, it is the self-liberating side of forgiveness that is frequently valued to the exclusion or the omission of the reconciling concern for the relationship. If I forgive another because resenting would be self-destructive, and withholding forgiveness would cut me off from right relationships with the One whose forgiveness is needed beyond all, I've missed the whole point. No matter how noble or splendid I may feel, it is not at all what Jesus intended. The goal of caring, of confrontation, of forgiveness is not self-salvation, it is reconciliation. The end intended is to regain the brother, to recover the sister, to restore the relationship (see Matt. 18:15).

Any view of forgiveness that focuses primarily on getting release for one's own conscience ("It's obviously not my problem, I've forgiven him"), escape from guilt ("It's clearly his attitude that separates us, I'm forgiving"), freedom from responsibility ("There's nothing more I can do than what I've done, he's forgiven"), is too easy, too cheap. The goal is community restored, not private perfection maintained.

When "forgiveness" ends open relationship, leaves people estranged, don't rush to it, it's not forgiveness; it's a face-saving, self-saving, time-saving escape.

Restoration Is the Goal

A 90-year-old veteran was being interviewed on the wisdom accumulated in a long life. "I'm 90 years old today and I don't have an enemy in the world," he said. The interviewer, hoping for a key insight, probed further. "What's your secret for living almost a century and not having an enemy?" "Easy," the old man replied, "I've outlived them all."

Forgiveness is the process of restoring relationships. Out-thinking, out-maneuvering, out-forgiving or out-living others is a dodge from the real goal. Forgiveness presses toward restoration. When what was estranged is brought back into fellowship again, when what was fragmented is whole again, when what was alienated is reunited, then forgiveness has come.

Torn from his home by 10 jealous older brothers, sold into slavery in Egypt—which is a living death, forgotten by those who once held him dear, Joseph sits in prison awaiting death. Instead, release, opportunity, elevation to prime minister follow. Then come the brothers asking for aid.

From the outset, Joseph's willingness to forgive is not in question, but his brothers' ability to receive it is. So he searches for a way to move them toward the place where forgiveness will mean anything to them beyond escape from retaliation. Joseph chooses to do everything possible to invite his brothers to a point where forgiveness can mean restored fellowship.

At last the brothers can admit their guilt, accept responsibility for their wrongdoing and express a change of heart that truly values another in genuine love. Then forgiveness becomes a bridge to restored fellowship among the brothers; or better said, open fellowship is for the first time achieved (see Gen. 37— 45).

Forgiveness opened the channels of trust, love, acceptance, and real brothering for the first time.

Community Is the Result

Created for, called to and recreated within community, we human beings require a continuous, dynamic process of maintaining that community with others. Forgiveness is that means to creative community. Forgiving is not an end in itself, but the opening of a self to join with other selves in loving community.

It is within community that we truly come to know God and to experience God's forgiveness. We cut ourselves off from the forgiving love of God when in begrudging another we cut off the brother who is God's channel for forgiveness, or shut out the sister who is the face of God to smile forgiveness, the voice of God to speak the word of forgiveness, the arms of God to receive us in reconciliation.

If we do not forgive our brother his trespasses, we will not be forgiven of God. The spirit of non-forgiveness becomes the blockade. The individualism of much privatistic protestantism has bypassed this and distorted forgiveness until it has become destructive of, rather than constructive of, community.

"God knows my heart, that I have truly forgiven, but I do not need to reapproach the other again."

"If my own heart is right, that is what matters most," is a private solution that eliminates the need for encountering God with my brother, through the other, in the present reality of the Body of Christ, called the church. So confession is taken to the closet, not to the opponent. It is expressed in prayer, not to the other party in the injury or conflict. "God and I have a good thing going on the side, I no longer need you to be the reality of Christ's Body to me."

The protestant principle of the priesthood of all believers is thus distorted to mean "every believer becomes his or her own priest." The biblical view is the reverse. Every believer can be and is the brother's or sister's priest. You, as priest, speak the word of forgiveness to me. I speak it for you. Forgiveness is only complete when we reach out to greet each other again.

The priority of forgiveness and reconciliation to worship and service cannot be made more clear than it is in the teachings of Jesus.

"If when you are bringing your gift to the altar, you suddenly remember that your brother has a grievance against you, leave your gift where it is before the altar.

First go and make your peace with your brother, and only then come back and offer your gift" (Matt. 5:23,24, *NEB*).

When "forgiveness" ends open relationship by promising a private release and an easier out, don't give it, don't accept it.

When "forgiveness" denies that there is anger, acts as if it never happened, and so blocks open relationship in community, don't trust it, don't settle for it.

When "forgiveness" foregoes repentance, and forgets the enduring unresolved issues of justice, don't rush to it, don't be taken in by it.

When "forgiveness" puts you one-up in a superior position, don't resolve it one-way, reach out equally, mutually, openly to be reconciled, to join in creative community.

Exploring the Biblical Basis

The goal of forgiving is the restoration and the celebration of Christian community in the Body of Christ. Forgiveness does not end but enriches relationship. For a condensed, focused passage of Scripture that presents this model precisely, examine Colossians 3:12-15 (see *RSV*).

Text	*Notes*
As God's chosen people, holy and beloved, put on compassion, kindness, put on meekness and patience, forbearing one another.	As God's new community of loving right relationships, be caring *with* each other, be supportive *of* each other,

If one has a complaint
   against another,
forgiving each other,
as the Lord has forgiven
   you
so you also must forgive.
And above all these
put on love
which binds everything
   together
in perfect harmony.
And let the peace of
   Christ
rule in your hearts
to which indeed you were
   called
in the one body.
And be thankful.

be accepting of each
   other,
be open, honest,
   confrontative,
working through to
   forgiveness.
Taking Christ as model,
   practice His loving
   integrity.
The crown, the goal, the
   objective, is loving
   relationship,
which connects us in
   balanced
complementarity,
in *pax Christos,* not *pax
   Romana,*
in inner wholeness,
in response to God,
in the body-life of
   community,
in grateful joy.

1. The passages on forgiveness in the New Testament focus on restored relationship, not on private peace with one's own individual conscience before God. (Do you agree, disagree, uncertain?)

2. Any solution that is not focused toward the re-creation or the procreation of community is abortive of the life-forming process, a miscarriage of community formation. (Are you agreed, disagreed, uncertain?)

3. Any "forgiveness" that ends ongoing relationship, reduces the possibilities for open communica-

tion, open confrontation, open covenanting of life together foregoes its true goals, forgets its essential purpose, does not forgive. (Agree, disagree, uncertain?)

For Further Experience
Personally and Small Group

Reflect on the following and affirm one behavioral goal (precise, concrete, measurable change for yourself on each).

1. I will not act as if I am "forgiving" by moving "one-up" or talking "one-down," in tense relationships. I will seek to stay level by . . .
2. I will not act unilaterally in private forgiving or individually in claiming the sole responsibility for a two-person problem. I will seek to stay mutual by . . .
3. I will not act neutral, nice, or non-feeling in avoiding genuineness or real contact with another in working through differences. I will seek new honesty by . . .
4. I will not use anger destructively when it can be expressed toward constructive and creative ends. I will act with new intensity by . . .
5. I will not despair of open healing in hurting relationships. I will seek wholeness, acceptance and deepened trust by . . .

Epilogue

On the Other Hand

Although in "forgiving", release unfortunately may be easier to achieve than reconciliation—

although one in error may choose to move over, away from, against the other—

although one in weakness may attempt to live off of, without, in spite of the other—

yet we dare not hesitate to take any step toward forgiving, no matter how faltering or fallible.

Yet we must not refuse to move toward another in seeking mutual repentance and renewed trust.

Yet we cannot despair of forgiveness and lose hope that reconciliation is possible.

CARING ENOUGH TO FORGIVE

True Forgiveness

David Augsburger

HERALD PRESS
Scottdale, Pennsylvania
Kitchener, Ontario

Scripture quotations in this publication are from the *RSV,
Revised Standard Version* of the Bible, copyright 1946 and
1952 by the Division of Christian Education of the NCCC,
U.S.A. and used by permission. Also the *NEB, The New
English Bible,* © The Delegates of the Oxford University Press
and the Syndics of the Cambridge University Press 1961,
1970. Reprinted by permission.

CARING ENOUGH TO FORGIVE
Copyright © 1981 by Regal Books

Herald Press edition published at Scottdale, PA. 15683

Released simultaneously in Canada by
Herald Press, Kitchener, Ont. N2G 4M5

Library of Congress Catalog Card No. 81-80913
International Standard Book Number: 0-8361-1965-7
Printed in the United States of America
83 84 85 86 87 10 9 8 7 6 5 4 3

In a world of
   flawed
communication,
community is possible
   through
   understanding
   others.

In a world of
   painful
   alienation,
community is created by
   accepting
   others.

In a world of
   broken
   trust,
community is sustained by
   forgiveness.

About the Author

David Augsburger is a forceful writer with a compassionate heart for the needs of people. He is well-
known across the nation for his award winning
radio broadcasts, and around the world for semi-
nars with the Mennonite Mission Board. With a
Ph.D. in pastoral psychotherapy and family therapy from the School of Theology at Claremont, Cali-
fornia, he is now professor of pastoral care at the
Associated Mennonite Biblical Seminaries in
Elkhart, Indiana. Dr. Augsburger has authored
many other books and has had hundreds of articles
published in magazines. This book is the second in
a new series of "Caring Enough" books by David
Augsburger.

Contents

Prologue

On the One Hand

No relationship exists long without tensions.

No community continues long without conflicts.

No human interaction occurs without the possibilities of pain, injury, suffering and alienation.

The hurts are always there. The misunderstandings inevitably happen. There is invariably trouble.

Without forgiveness, community is only possible where people are safely and cautiously superficial.

With forgiveness, we are set free to meet genuinely, to interact authentically, to risk being fully present with each other in integrity.

Such forgiveness draws people toward each other. It comes to terms with the past, then allows it to truly be past. It opens the future but does not determine it so that people are unable to be living, free and spontaneous again. It deals clearly with the present in true repentance, change and growth.

Such forgiveness is more than a benevolent act of superior generosity, or a sacrificial act of one-way absorbing of the other's debt, or an obedient act of unconditional acceptance. Each of these views emerges from a different understanding of what love is, of what agape is, of what discipleship is, of who comprises community.

The biblical love, which is called *agape*, is equal regard. Such regard is then benevolent, sacrificial, obedient, and it is even more than these—it is also just. It leads to a forgiveness which is "the mutual recognition that repentance is genuine, and right (righteous) relationships are now achieved." Such forgiveness is the final form of love which results in renewed and reconciled community.

I see you
   as a wrongdoer.

I feel
   injured,
   innocent,
   exploited,
   abused.

I am
   pointing the finger of
   blame.

Any movement toward
   forgiving begins with
   recognizing that
   we are in this pain
   together.

1 ■ Forgive

By Realizing Wrongdoing

"I trusted that man. I once said I'd trust him with my life or my wife. I escaped with my life, but that's all.

"We belonged to the same church, the same social group. He had a good practice as a therapist—until I fixed it for him. I was the one who insisted we go for counseling, Jill and me. He preferred to see us individually. When she told me she was moving out and moving in with him, I didn't believe it. Not until I saw them going into his apartment together.

"I have never hated anyone as much as I did him. Even after my attorney had filed all the briefs and he lost his license to practice because of unethical behavior, I still hated him.

"It's four years now, and I'm no better. Just the

thought of her and my stomach is tight with pain and loneliness. One glimpse of him on the street and I'm ruined for the day. He did me wrong. He did us wrong. Now, we're no longer 'us.' In some ways my life ended then, and I can't let go of the memories; I can't go on alone."

"I've Been Wronged"

How does one deal with the pain, anger and injustice felt when wronged by another?

First, by reducing the sense of outraged innocence. When angry, most human beings prefer to see the other as the invader, attacker, exploiter, and the self as the innocent victim. Maintaining this definition frees the self from blame and responsibility while laying it solely at the other's doorstep.

However, such one-sided injustices are rare among continuing relationships. There are hit-and-run acts of one-way violation of another in which one person is obviously the offender, and this is recognized by both. But in most situations of interpersonal pain, particularly those that occur in the midst of friendships, marriages, work relationships or communities, the ratios of responsibility that are assigned show a part of the problem belongs to either and to both.

For example, look again at the opening case history. The speaker presents evidence to show that the other two persons in the triangle are obviously the wrongdoers, he has been "done wrong." But look again. The marriage in trouble was a union of two people. When the relationship falters, both are responsible. When one partner is open to an outside alliance, both are involved in the

**Multiple Choice
in any Situation
of "Perceived Wrongdoing"
There are an infinite number of ways
of assigning
responsibility**

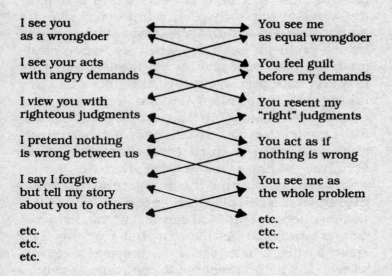

I see you
as a wrongdoer

You see me
as equal wrongdoer

I see your acts
with angry demands

You feel guilt
before my demands

I view you with
righteous judgments

You resent my
"right" judgments

I pretend nothing
is wrong between us

You act as if
nothing is wrong

I say I forgive
but tell my story
about you to others

You see me as
the whole problem

etc.
etc.
etc.

etc.
etc.
etc.

FIGURE 1

death of their covenant through infidelity. And
when the partner is a mutually selected friend,
someone is closing his eyes to what is taking place.
Both are responsible to some degree.

There are infinite combinations of these
amounts of responsibility to be distributed among
all who participate in any situation of pain.

"You're to Blame"

Obviously it is of little value to fix blame,
although the impulse to try seems to spring eter-
nally in most. The only useful function is to blow
the cover of our own pseudo-innocence. We are
both involved in our disagreements. It takes two to
have a problem. Each of us can see, when clear-
eyed, the part each plays; even though your part
may only have been a failure to recognize that I was
taking you for granted—so you feel used, or a
choice to overlook another's growing irresponsibil-
ity—so you feel exploited, or a refusal to talk openly
about differences until the other blew up in
accumulated anger—so you feel attacked.

Even when the bind that is creating frustration
in another is a part of the whole community system
which I accept readily, I am a part of the other
person's problem. As I accept that part, however
small a slice it may seem in comparison to the
whole, I am better prepared to confront the wrongdoing without affront. The willingness to appreci-
ate and own my part must, of course, be a sincere
recognition of shared participation in the pain of
life experiences, and not a strategy to induce guilt,
invite an apology or a confession from the other, or
to evade the seriousness of the facts or acts in the

strained relationship. The purpose of authentic identification is to restore perceptions of love. The goal is real contact in honest recognition of things as they are. Love is an end in itself since it sees the other as an end, not as a means. Thus any step of loving identification is not a means to manipulate the other to move back into relation and make things right according to my prescription. Loving identification is its own reward, its own justification, its own reason for being.

The initial step in dealing with the intense feelings of being wronged, and the confirmed conviction that the other is the sole wrongdoer, is to give up the attitude of injured innocence and stand alongside once more in loving identification.

"But It Isn't My Fault"

"I didn't leave her, she left me. I did not want our marriage to break up. I was committed to her, faithful to her; I still haven't given her up, even though she's been living with her therapist for almost a year now. If I could have done anything more, believe me I would have. But I couldn't think, choose or love for her. She had to do that for herself. The responsibility for what she did is at her doorstep. She is to blame for ending our marriage, not me."

The need to place blame resides very close to the moral center of a person. When an injustice has been done, an evil act committed, responsibility gets assigned in a conscious attempt to create justice out of injustice or in an unconscious desire to even the ledgers of justice that are deep within each of us. This urgency for justice emerges early in childhood development. With the learning of "right and wrong" ways of thinking, choosing and acting during the second, third and fourth years, a demand for fairness is created. Of all the primal demands which spring from the core of early childhood learnings, none is more persistent in its continuing power; none is more insistent in its demands for having an injury satisfied or rectified; and none is more consistent from early stages until the final experiences of life.

These voices for justice rise automatically in one's inner court. "It isn't my fault," one insists instantly when unfairly accused. "It's certainly his fault," one's inner judge asserts when another is seen as a wrongdoer.

Working for justice is a lifelong task, and it is better done by the more mature process of assessing guilt and defining responsibility than by the earlier process of shame and blame.

The earliest process for working out such imbalances is to feel shame and to place blame. These begin in the second year of life and continue until one matures to the next level of thinking and responding. Shame is the sense of total rejection, utter confusion, complete exposure before rejecting others. It is the feeling of being found out, uncovered, on the spot, and motivates one to hide. It is a feeling of being blamed and of needing to displace that blame onto another.

In later childhood, when a conscience is taking clear shape, an internal judge who can define guilt in more sharply focused forms begins to direct the inner responses to conflictive feelings.

Guilt is a feeling in response to a specific act, to an inappropriate behavior, to a violated value. It leads one to admit to the wrong act, to confess, to seek forgiveness. Its central focus is on responsibility, not blame.

"So Where Do We Begin?"

Significant movement toward forgiving begins as we bring an end to blaming and move toward the recognition of our joint participation, to whatever degree, in the painful situation. Blaming seeks to finger the culprit, assign the role of villain, and proceed to exacting a commensurate punishment. (All of which are negative alienating acts that increase rather than reduce distance.)

This cuts across a whole layer of fantasies that spring up when hurt feelings reign:

The fantasy that pointing the finger of blame with angry finality will help reduce the pain.

The fantasy that repeating a magical ritual apology, like "I'm so sorry, please forgive me" will release one from the binding misunderstandings.

The fantasy that undoing can redo the situation. ("I'll make it up to you" or "I'll atone by doing some great service for someone else" or "I'll just act nice in the future to show my heart is right.")

The fantasy that avoidance ("if we don't talk about it, it won't hurt so much") or denial (problem? what problem?) will ease the situation and make it easier for us to reconcile.

The fantasy that displacing the pressure by gossiping the tension to someone else, or taking out the frustration on someone else, or ventilating the anger on some person, place or thing will be useful in getting us back together again.

All of these fantasies are ways of dodging blame

or depositing blame at another's feet. Ending blame is the better step. Taking sole responsibility for one's own part in clearly expressed words and respecting the other's full responsibility for his or her part allows both to see the wrongdoing for what it truly is, without enlarging the field of misunderstanding until it is unmanageable.

In any situation of perceived wrongdoing, constructive relating is not possible as long as these perceptions of wrongdoing are held between us.

If I see you as a wrongdoer, regardless of the accuracy of my perceptions, I will not be able to respond fairly or relate openly until I have dealt responsibly with the injury I have suffered, the irritation I feel, or the indignation I am carrying. No strategy of avoidance and denial, no game of magical words or actions of undoing, no exercise of punitive blaming or displacement in gossip will offer any help or healing. I need to work through the difference with you if at all possible, and with some trustworthy brother or sister if the encounter is not possible—as in the case of another's severe illness or death.

Wrongdoing cannot be avoided or evaded. It simply is, and must be faced.

Jesus says, "If you have something against your brother" (see Matt. 18:15) or "if your brother has something against you" (see Matt. 5:23,24) go and win right relationships with the other again. Such reconciliation must precede service, worship, and personal acts of response to God; for only the forgiving spirit is open to the divine Spirit.

Wrongdoing is not a valid reason for my not seeing you as a person of worth.

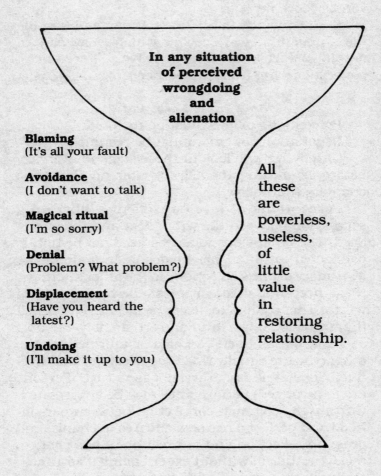

**In any situation
of perceived
wrongdoing
and
alienation**

Blaming
(It's all your fault)

Avoidance
(I don't want to talk)

Magical ritual
(I'm so sorry)

Denial
(Problem? What problem?)

Displacement
(Have you heard the
 latest?)

Undoing
(I'll make it up to you)

All
these
are
powerless,
useless,
of
little
value
in
restoring
relationship.

FIGURE 2

Wrongdoing is not a just basis for my not seeing you as a fellow human of infinite value.

Wrongdoing is no justification for my not loving you as I love myself.

Besides, we are in this—to some extent, in some measure, and in ways beyond which I may want to admit—we are in this together. We will need help, concern, caring from each other.

"So What Is Forgiving?"

Perceptions of love must be restored.

Negotiations of trust must be resumed.

(Briefly, we will look at these steps in overview before examining them in greater depth in the chapters that follow.)

Perceptions of love can make a liberating separation between the wrongdoer and the wrong deed. The other's preciousness need not be tightly connected to his or her behavior. In spite of the legitimacy of one's objections to the other's actions, these need not shape or misshape perceptions of worth. The freedom to disconnect these for oneself (I am precious, worthful and irreducibly valuable as I am, not as I act) can also be affirmed for the other (you are equally worthful, precious, and irreducibly valuable as you are, not as you act). Persons are to be prized, performance may be appreciated. Cutting the common connection between personhood and performance sets one free to change and grow, to reflect on and redirect one's behavior, to receive criticism without experiencing it as attack, to constantly transcend the present moment and become more than I have been in the preceding one.

In Forgiving

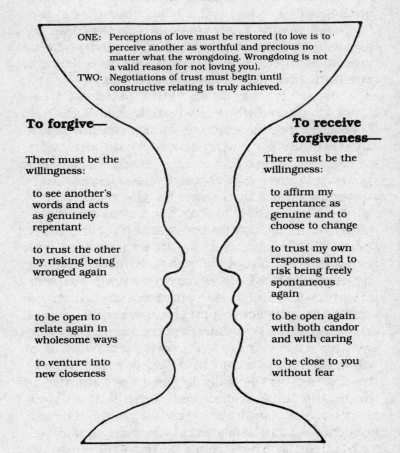

ONE: Perceptions of love must be restored (to love is to perceive another as worthful and precious no matter what the wrongdoing. Wrongdoing is not a valid reason for not loving you).

TWO: Negotiations of trust must begin until constructive relating is truly achieved.

To forgive—

There must be the willingness:

to see another's words and acts as genuinely repentant

to trust the other by risking being wronged again

to be open to relate again in wholesome ways

to venture into new closeness

To receive forgiveness—

There must be the willingness:

to affirm my repentance as genuine and to choose to change

to trust my own responses and to risk being freely spontaneous again

to be open again with both candor and with caring

to be close to you without fear

FIGURE 3

As perceptions of love are restored, the wrong-doing can now be seen for what it is—a wrong choice to take a wrong action in a wrong direction. The anger can be focused on the behavior, not the one misbehaving. Both anger and love become an invitation for the person to own what has been done without defense or denial and move toward repentant change. Acceptance of the person is now kept distinct from approval of that person's intentions or actions. One can stand truly with the other while standing fully for one's values, commitments and convictions, as negotiations of trust are begun again.

Trust is severed in an interpersonal crisis, and it stands frozen until conversations can be resumed. Negotiations of trust are a constant intermingling of risking openness and trusting in response which then leads to further openness and increased trust. Trust and risk go hand in hand. So the conversations for clarifying intentions and affirming new directions can work out mutual repentance until each is perceived as genuine.

This process is equally demanding for the giver and the receiver of forgiveness. Each requires a willingness to both trust and risk. For the forgiver, there must be the willingness to see another's words and acts as genuinely repentant so that suspicion and mindreading are laid aside, the past is dismissed, and the present transaction is made with integrity. There must be the willingness to trust the other by risking being wronged again, even though the person wrongs you repeatedly, "seven times in the day," Jesus said (Luke 17:4, *RSV*). That's every hour on the hour. And for those who keep score, multiply it even more (see Matt. 18:22).

There must be the willingness to be open to new ways of relating, new experiments in being more real with each other because of the ground gained by the hurt and the healing.

Receiving forgiveness is an equal risk. In accepting forgiveness from another, there must be the willingness to affirm clearly and candidly that my repentance is genuine and that I am choosing to change. There must be a willingness to trust my own responses and to risk being freely spontaneous again even as I know that this could lead to my repeating the failure and reopening the wound.

There must also be the willingness to be open again with both candor and caring. I will not be inhibited by past failure and timid about contributing to our relationship lest failure follow failure and my repentance be questioned as inadequate and insincere. Forgiveness allows me to risk being myself fully and freely. So I can be close to you without fear, moving back into intimacy without anxiety shooting up and paralyzing my ability to be near you.

These are the steps that lead to our mutual recognition that intentions and new directions are genuine in authentic repenting, and right relationships are now either restored or achieved.

And this is forgiving.

Exploring the Biblical Basis
Matthew 18:23-35 contains the most profound story of true and false forgiving. Let's examine it in

dramatic form to gain the impact of Jesus' argument.

Scene 1: The time is the early part of the first century. The place is the countryside of Galilee.

Prologue: Peter has just asked the question, "7?" Jesus answers, "70 x 7!" Then He tells the following story.

Act One

The Ten-Million-Dollar Man

It is inventory day in the king's palace. All accounts are due. Among them is "A" who owes 10 million dollars and cannot pay. The king orders him sold out, including sale of man, wife, children into slavery to gain settlement.

The man pleads, "Lord, have patience with me and I will pay you everything." Out of pity, the king releases him and forgives him his debt.

Act Two

The Twenty-Dollar Debtor

As he walks out of the courtroom, the Ten-Million-Dollar Man runs into friend "B," a 20-dollar debtor. Throttling him, he demands, "Pay me what you owe."

"Have patience. I will pay you."

"Nothing doing," he replies and has him thrown into debtor's prison until he comes up with the 20.

Act Three

Life Imprisonment

The friends of both who saw this take place were very distressed, and they reported all to the king. "You wicked servant! I forgave you all that debt at your request. Should you not have had mercy on your fellow servant as I had mercy on you?" In anger, the king delivered him to the torturers until he had paid all.

Epilogue: "So also my heavenly Father will do to every one of you, if you do not forgive your brother from your heart" (v. 35, RSV).

1. The proper issue is not Peter's question, "How often shall my brother sin against me, and I forgive him? As many as seven times?" But, "As a multiple offender myself, dare I withhold forgiveness from a repentant person even once?"

2. The king "released him" from present angry demands and "forgave him the debt." Two merciful acts: The first restored freedom, the second repaid indebtedness. Both are important. The first deals with demands for loving. The second with demands for living with what he is and with what he has or hasn't.

3. The king allowed the man to receive the

identical sentence he had prescribed for another. God allows us to receive upon ourselves what we seek to impose upon another. Compare this with 2 Samuel 12:1-23 and Esther 7:1-10 for parallels in Jewish literature.

4. Read Mark 11:25 as a parallel commentary: "And whenever you stand praying, forgive, if you have anything against any one; so that your Father also who is in heaven may forgive you your trespasses" (*RSV*).

For Further Experience

PERSONAL
Choose among the following for reflection:
1. *On blaming*
_____ A. When there is wrongdoing my immediate reaction is to find out *who's* wrong and fix blame
_____ B. When there is wrong done, my immediate response is to find out *what's* wrong and assign responsibility
_____ C. When there is wrong between us, my choice is to find out *how* things went wrong and how we can get things right between us again
_____ D. When things go wrong, I do all of the above or combinations of the above in sequence
_____ E. None of the above. Problem? What problem?
2. *On fantasy*
When there is wrongdoing, my preferred fantasy is:

_____ A. Ritual apology resolves all, "I'm so sorry"

_____ B. Punishing someone will reduce the pain

_____ C. Undoing can redo the situation by making it up to the other in kindness

_____ D. Avoidance helps, "Let's not discuss it"

_____ E. Displacement works. "I'll talk to someone else, perhaps that will help"

3. *On forgiving*

When forgiving, my most difficult point of working through is:

_____ A. I find it hard to restore perceptions of love

_____ B. I hold back from working at renewing trust

_____ C. I hesitate to see the other's repentance as genuine

_____ D. I am cautious about risking being wronged again

_____ E. I am not easily open to venturing close again

4. *On receiving forgiveness*

When receiving forgiveness I find the hardest part is in:

_____ A. Accepting love when I feel shame or guilt

_____ B. Willingness to affirm that my repentance is genuine

_____ C. Willingness to trust my own spontaneous responses again

_____ D. Venturing to be open again with candor and caring

_____ E. Risking closeness again without fear.

IN SMALL GROUP

Using the above exercises, invite group members to reflect on which of the options best express their own tension points on handling blame, fantasies, and in giving and receiving forgiveness.

Listen to each other's self-disclosure without probing, evaluating or interpreting. Then ask if there is any point where group help would be appreciated. If so, then offer insights from around the circle, but with respect for the receiver's right to accept, refuse or use in part the ideas and experiences offered.

I see you
   as an evildoer.

I feel
   hurt, resentful, angry,
   demanding.

I am refusing to see you
   as an equally precious
   person of
   worth,
   value,
   dignity—
   in spite of wrongdoing.

Forgiveness begins
   as I see you again
with love.

2 ■ Forgive

By Reaffirming Love

"I hate my brother-in-law," the woman said. "I cannot forgive him for what he did to my sister. Although he is respected as a community leader, I will never be able to trust him again.

"Year after year, he chipped away at her self-esteem, undermining her self-image until she had lost all confidence in her own ability to think for herself or to trust her own feelings. I will never be able to forgive him for that.

"They married when she was just becoming her own person. She was so much in love she did not see that he was quickly taking over her whole personality. He spoke for her, restating her ideas in more eloquent words when she did speak. Before long, he thought, felt, chose for her, and all in such helpful ways that she felt insensitive to object.

"After their first child, she began to withdraw all the more. He became even more helpful and over-responsible until she was all but absorbed and overwhelmed by periods of depression. Even worse, she felt guilty that she was not on top of everything as he appeared to be.

"Now, after she has been getting therapy for her problems, he still refuses to see how he helped to slowly turn her into a non-person. When I have pointed out that it takes two to create such a depressive relationship, one to be depressed and one to be depressing, he just becomes all the more helpful, nice and sacrificial. He looks martyred when I point out that he shares in the problem.

"So I stay away from their place unless I know he's gone. I can't and I won't see it his way, that it's all her problem. I can't look at him without feeling the hatred welling up in me. There's no way I can accept him as a brother again."

One Step at a Time

Forgiveness, which is a complex and demanding process, is often reduced to a single act of accepting another. In spite of the pain, hurt, loss and wrongdoing that stand between us, we are encouraged to forgive in a single act of resolving all by giving unconditional inclusion. Such a step becomes too large for any human to take in a single bound. Forgiveness is a journey of many steps, each of which can be extremely difficult, all of which are to be taken carefully, thoughtfully, and with deep reflection.

Rather than a single step, a whole flight of steps

Forgiveness is
the final form of love

STEP 1. To see the other as having worth again, regardless of wrongdoing

— VALUING ———→

Is this forgiveness? No, it is the prerequesite love.

STEP 2. To see the other as equally precious again, in spite of the pain felt

— LOVING ———→

Is this then forgiveness? No, it is the requisite first step.

STEP 3. To cancel demands on the past, recognizing that changing the unchangeable is impossible

— CANCELING DEMANDS ─→

Is this forgiveness? No, this is coming to terms with reality. No, it is the reality which undergirds it.

STEP 4. To work through the anger and pain felt by both in reciprocal trusting and risking until genuineness in intention is perceived and repentance is seen by both to be authentic

— TRUSTING NOW ———→

Is this forgiveness? Yes, forgiving is now being done.

STEP 5. To drop the demands for an ironclad guarantee of future behavior and open the future to choice, to spontaneity, to the freedom to fail again.

— OPENING THE FUTURE →

Is this forgiveness? Yes, this is the central work of forgiving.

STEP 6. To touch each other deeply, to feel moved in warmth, love, compassion, to celebrate it in mutual recognition that right relationships have been achieved.

— CELEBRATING LOVE ───→

And this? This is the bonding, celebrating.

FIGURE 4

confront us if forgiveness is to truly occur. Each builds on what precedes; each makes possible that which follows.

Step one moves from devaluing the wrongdoer to *valuing* the person again. The second step advances from the neutral recognition of the other's worth to a return to *loving* the other as a precious person again. Then the past must be recognized as past through *canceling* demands for undoing. Then present anger, pain or sadness must be negotiated in renewed *trusting*. This allows both parties to risk *opening* the future again and to reward each other in *celebrating* the new understanding and love achieved.

Each of these steps is an integral part of the forgiving process, although the first three are loving steps, not truly forgiving steps. As the basic prerequisites for beginning the work of forgiving, they are indispensable. But when the process ends with restored perceptions of value, love and respect for the reality of what has happened, then the heart of authentic forgiveness has not been understood or experienced. The fact that the most widely used definitions of forgiveness offer little more than these prerequisite steps, awakens deep concern in those who value reconciliation and the restoration of community, for the real work of forgiving is not just the release from hatred, resentment, suspicion, and hostility in the forgiver, it is found in regaining the sister and brother as a full sister, as a true brother.

Valuing and Loving Is Where We Begin
"I hate my brother-in-law," the woman said. "I

cannot forgive him, respect him, accept him as a brother again."

Perhaps she can. If real concern for her sister is to be expressed in a way that calls out change, growth and a renewed identity, it must begin with a choice to value self and other with equal regard. As long as she is doing her sister's hating for her, feeling her sister's unfelt anger, acting out her sister's frustration, feeling her sister's feelings in her behalf, she will be of no lasting help. Only when she lets her sister face her own conflicts will she stop doing the same rescuing as the man she now hates. (It is not our differences that cause most of our anger problems, it is our similarities. The person that truly rankles my feelings of rejection or rage is the one who is obviously abusing another in the way I am seeking to repress, deny or correct myself.)

She is of little use to her sister until she stops carrying a vendetta for her and lets her work out her own pain and injustice. But she can be of significant help to both of them if she makes a genuine contact with each that allows her to express her own feelings (not her sister's), her own concerns (not secondhand messages being carried from person to person), and works out her own relationship with her and with him.

Only when she has begun to value each of them as persons of worth, no matter how deeply she may disagree with either's behavior, will she be able to offer anything of real use. Then when perceptions of love have been restored, communication can be resumed and open conversation on trusting can be risked again. Can she trust them to be honest with her now? The brother-in-law's past absorbing behaviors cannot be changed. What has happened is out of reach. The sister's past submission is now history. It cannot be recalled. Demands that the past be recalled, recycled, rewritten and revised are fantasy demands. They are not possible and are of no value to giver or receiver. The sooner they are canceled, the better (the better to love another again).

When the other can be seen as a person of equal worth with the self, in spite of the objectionable actions, then the possibility of reconciliation and redemptive change comes back into view. Love makes it possible for us to see, think, feel, want and act differently toward another again; but love becomes possible as all of these elements are exercised in responding positively toward the other once more.

Seeing, Thinking, Feeling, Intending, Acting

Love is the whole response of the whole person to another who is seen in equal wholeness. But loving begins as a part, not the whole, in one element of the process and then spreads throughout the whole series of responses which make up the human person.

Loving can begin in an exercise of any part of the whole cycle of seeing—thinking—feeling—intending—acting, and then gradually affects the whole.

For example, acting is a way to evoke affectionate feelings. If we are trapped in a stalled elevator together and act to reassure, support, aid each other, those actions will evoke new ways of seeing, thinking, feeling and intending. An incidental

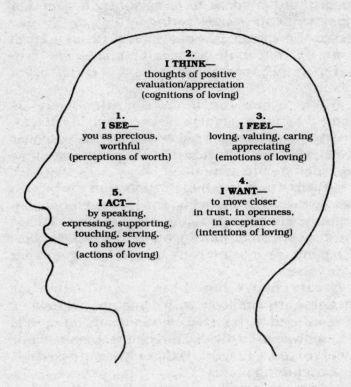

2.
I THINK—
thoughts of positive
evaluation/appreciation
(cognitions of loving)

1.
I SEE—
you as precious,
worthful
(perceptions of worth)

3.
I FEEL—
loving, valuing, caring
appreciating
(emotions of loving)

5.
I ACT—
by speaking,
expressing, supporting,
touching, serving,
to show love
(actions of loving)

4.
I WANT—
to move closer
in trust, in openness,
in acceptance
(intentions of loving)

Awareness can break through at any point in the cycle.
I may *feel* love first and know what I *want* before I am
aware of how I *see* you or what my *thoughts* are.

Or I may be *thinking* critically and not be aware that I
am *seeing* you as a threat to my safety, and this is
triggering my *feelings* of dislike, etc., etc., etc.

FIGURE 5

opportunity to speak to or speak up for another
most frequently evokes caring feelings for the one
served. No sooner has one spoken up in a small
group to contribute an idea or take some own-
ership in the process than feelings of caring begin
to stir.

Or note how intentions can stimulate emotions. When one is lonely, isolated, and looking for
a person to converse with, even a neutral response
arouses hope and begins to evoke positive feelings
and elicit further action.

When caring, trusting relationships are broken
by a perceived wrongdoing, the loving relationship
begins again with changing how I see you. This is
the most available, more possible and usually effective point for moving back toward loving another
once more.

I can change how I see you. Although my
thoughts are conflicted with demands, my feelings
are confused with mixed emotions, my intentions
are ambivalent in divided directions, I can redefine
how I see you. Often this is the only change possible
as a beginning point.

Awareness can break through at any point in
the cycle.

I may *feel* love first and know what I *want* before
I am aware of how I *see* you or what my *thoughts*
are.

Or I may be *thinking* critically and not be aware
that I am *seeing* you as a threat to my safety, and
this is triggering my *feelings* of dislike, etc., etc.,
etc.

I cannot alter my thinking without denying one
pole or the other in my contrasting evaluations of

the person I see as a wrongdoer, or without distorting my thoughts on something less than honesty.

I cannot directly transform my feelings since I am only indirectly in control of my emotions. My emotions are the energy content of my perceptions and evaluations. They change as I view you in new ways, or value you in new respect; but I cannot redirect my feelings at will. I can and do choose how I see you in this moment, so I am responsible for my feelings and able to respond with new feelings from moment to moment.

So as I choose how I see you, I can clarify my positive thoughts toward you, awaken positive feelings about you, direct my intentions toward deepening relationship with you and choose to move toward you again.

Seeing Your Equal Worth

To perceive you as equally precious again requires that I see myself as precious, worthful, irreducibly valuable as a person; or my equal regard may be expressed in my despising you as equally worthless.

I am irreducibly valuable simply because, and only because I am I. You are irreducibly valuable solely because, and wholly because you are you. No superabundance of good behavior, outstanding performance, or admirable appearance will increase your worth, nor will the reverse reduce your worth. I, you, we are irreducible in value, for we are created in the image of God. This image is not a likeness that I possess as an individual, for being in the image of God is clearly appraised as the state *we* express as persons in relationship, in community, in unity with each other before God. So the image is in our maleness AND femaleness, in our person-hood AND our peoplehood, in our singleness AND in our solidarity. My worth is grounded in my being a part of God's worthful creation called humanity. My preciousness is experienced truly when I stand in right relationships with others, reverencing their equal worth in equal regard. (See Gen. 1:27,28; 5:1,2; Eph. 4:23,24.)

Four attitudes toward valuing of self and other have predominated the thinking of Christians for the past two thousand years:

One, affirmation of the other and negation of the self (love of neighbor is a virtue, love of self a vice).

Two, affirmation of the other, toleration of the self (neighbor-love is the one true service; self-love is acceptable only for maintenance so that I will not be a burden to the loved neighbor).

Three, self-love and neighbor-love are both vir-tues (one must learn to love self as a basis for truly loving the neighbor).

Four, neighbor-love and self-love are two aspects of one and the same love. (No distinction, no separation, no sequence of priority are possible since true love of self and other are simultaneous expressions of the recognition of our equal, essen-tial, irreducible worth before God and with each other.)

The basis for reaffirming perceptions of love for another who is seen as a wrongdoer is the profound awareness that I-you-we are of infinite worth, in spite of, apart from, with no dependence on appear-ance, performance, effectiveness or any other ex-ternal criteria.

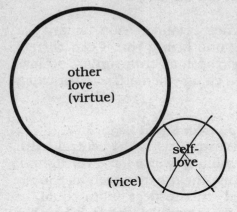

View one
Love of neighbor is
praiseworthy
Love of self is the
essential sin

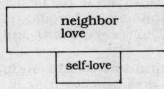

View two
Neighbor love is our
task
Self-love a necessary
maintenance

View three
Neighbor love and
self-love are equal in
value, virtue,
importance. Self-love
precedes, makes the
other possible

View four
Neighbor love and
self-love are two
aspects of the same
love. They are
indivisible,
irreducible, one.

FIGURE 6

Wrongdoing is not a valid reason for my not valuing, respecting and loving you. I can correct and redirect my perceptions from unlove to love when angry or when calm, when attracted or when repulsed.

Seeing You with Equal Regard

Love is equal regard. This is the central truth expressed in the biblical word for love, *agape.* Agape is offered when the other is seen as equally worthful, or treated with respect as an equal, or heard as a person with equal rights to his or her opinions, or honored as a human with equal responsibility for his or her choices, emotions and actions.

Throughout two millenniums of Christian theology, love—agape love—has been seen in incredibly varied ways: as benevolence, as obedience, as sacrifice, as equal regard.

As kind benevolence, agape-love is viewed as loving the unlovely and the unlovable. The fact that such a view belittles the beloved is overlooked since the lover has a clear vision of what could be made of the other if the love is effective in working its desired change. (Nonsense. Another may be unloving toward me, but that does not make that one unlovable.)

As simple obedience, agape-love is seen as loving another because I know I should, because I feel I ought. The fact that loving another out of a sense of obligation stimulates feelings of resistance in the one giving the love, and resentment from the one receiving such grudging acceptance, is overlooked in the flush of good feelings from being good and loving.

As self-sacrifice, agape-love is envisioned as sacrificing the self for the sake of others, as offering "you come first, your happiness is my chief reward, your welfare will require the loss of mine, but it is of no consequence.

"Such self-sacrifice is frequently its own reward as the giver is privileged with a glorious sense of righteousness and sacrificial superiority even in taking an inferior position in voluntary self-negation.

As equal-regard, agape-love is expressed in valuing the other as equally worthy of respect, rights and responsibility before God and before others.

In forgiving, benevolent-forgiveness offers one-up or one-way forgiving that gently reminds the other of who is doing the forgiving in this situation as in most others.

Obedient-forgiveness extends firm and faithful respect, but the heart is not there since getting it right is often more important than gaining the sister or the brother.

Sacrificial-forgiveness yields in forgiving by absorbing the pain, accepting the hurt, bearing the anger of both self and other and setting the other free with no strings attached, no questions asked, no real equality or mutuality asked for or expected, and no truly open and trusting relationship achieved.

Equal regard seeks forgiveness that is as mutual, as reciprocal, as equal in trust, risk, openness, and willingness to welcome what the future may bring as is possible for the persons involved.

Equal regard, as the expression of agape, is a loving concern for the dignity of persons considered as ends in themselves. An injury most often results in the instant severing of the relationship of agape, and forgiveness recognizes the actuality of the wrongdoing, reaffirms the loving concern of an equal regard and proceeds to the restoration of the relationship. Thus agapaic forgiveness is perception, emotion and action: the other is perceived as precious again, valued in loving concern, and confronted with the issues of restoring trusting relationships once more.

Exploring the Biblical Basis

Let's trace the thread of teaching about agape-love as it runs through the Bible. Read each of these teachings one after another to notice how they stack insight on insight into the nature of real loving.

Leviticus 19:15-18: In matters of justice, of gossip, of acting as a witness, in dealing with hatred, with wrongdoing, with anger, the central principle is "you shall love your neighbor as yourself" and this is based on the equal value the Creator has placed upon us. "I am Yahweh."

Matthew 22:39; 19:19; Mark 12:31; Luke 10:27: In daily life, in respect for others, in fulfilling God's highest intentions for us, we love our neighbor as ourselves and in doing this we are showing our love for God with our whole heart, soul, strength and mind—recognizing the authority of the One who said, "I am Yahweh."

John 15:34,35; 15:9-14: In caring for others as equally precious, we do not draw lines to say how far our love will go. Jesus drew no lines, even unto death. He said God draws no lines (see Matt. 5:43-

48). Like our Master, we love equally like the God who said, "I am Yahweh."

Romans 13:9; Galatians 5:14; James 2:8; Ephesians 5:28,29: In all of life, equal regard is the basis for living justly, prizing others truly, and serving joyfully. Equal regard is love.

Now reflect on what you have read. Notice that agape-love is kind, benevolent, obedient and self-sacrificial because it values others as equal in worth, in importance, in preciousness as persons.

For Further Experience

PERSONAL

1. Love is expressed in each stage of the awareness cycle. Reflect on difficulties experienced in each:
   ____ A. Seeing. I find it hard/easy to see another as precious again after an experience of pain.
   ____ B. Thinking. I think conflicting/critical thoughts about another which makes it hard to respect the other as a valued person after I have been hurt.
   ____ C. Feeling. I struggle with mixed feelings for a while before I can begin caring again.
   ____ D. Willing. I experience a divided will. One side wants to reach out, the other to withdraw or to get even.
   ____ E. Acting. I find it hard to put my caring into words, or to demonstrate it in action, or to return deeds of loving.
2. Now rephrase these items to match your own tension points and express your difficulties in restoring perceptions, thoughts, feelings, will, and actions of love.

3. Plan one new action for the next seven days that will rehearse and practice a new way of responding to a hurtful situation. For example: "This week, whenever I think of D. A. I will see him as equally a precious person as myself and visualize the core of his personhood as a gift of God, despite behaviors of which I disapprove."

IN SMALL GROUP

1. You may choose to do the preceding exercise around the circle, reporting on the point of difficulty and choosing one significant new behavior in response to this "stuck point."

2. Or you may seat five people in a circle as a fishbowl in the center of the group. Assign one of the five awareness functions to each person. Using exercise 1 in the "Personal" section for a thumbnail description—or the diagram, figure 5—consider these five awareness-function persons as making up a composite person. Now invite people from the outer circle to present a problem to this "composite person" and have each part respond in sequence, starting with "I see," etc. For deeper insight, present a problem first to Mr. Feeling or to Ms. Will and note how difficult response can be until observation (I see), cognition (I think), and emotion (I feel) have supplied their information. Or do skips from one to five, like a kid in a candy shop with no impulse control, or from three to five like an angry person popping off with temper.

3. Now reflect together how all of the self is involved in loving as equal regard expressed in true agape.

The past exists
  only in
  memory,
  consequences,
  effects.

It has power
  over me only as
  I continue to
  give it my power.

I can
  let go,
  release it,
  move freely.
I am not my past.
The future is not yet.

I can
  fear it,
  flee it,
  face it,
  embrace it,
and be free to live now.

3 ■ Forgive

By Releasing the Past

I am feeling resentment. Memories of a past injury are flooding my mind. My forehead is furrowed, my teeth clenched, my eyes narrowed. My thoughts are cyclical, repeating phrases, demands, accusations, and pointing imaginary fingers of blame. I'm not even here where I sit in my chair. I'm back in a painful moment of the past, facing a situation that no longer exists and acting as though the past were real, actual, present, here, now. I am holding it close in pain.

"Enough of that," I decide. Suddenly I'm feeling suspicion and fear as I sit looking around the airport where I am stranded by an air controller's strike. The past has disappeared for the moment, and I'm wondering about my possibilities of getting home. Doubts about the airline's honesty, predictions (anything which can go wrong, will go wrong) are being repeated as I brood. I'm wandering through my fantasies and fears about the future. The frustrations of canceling out tomorrow's schedule, and above all, the disappointment I share with Nancy by phone when I tell her I won't be on the evening flight, evoke a series of negative feelings. I'm holding back from the future with suspicious fears.

I pause and look around the large room at the people passing. A child cries, the mother slaps him, twice. The sound is sharp even amid all the noise. I feel sadness for them both. Beyond them two people are crying, saying good-bye. I see them holding on to each other, holding back the moment of parting.

I am like them. I am holding on to the past—but in resentment. I am holding back from the future in suspicion; I am refusing to be here now, present and fully alive. If I am willing to let go of the past without trying to change the unchangeable, and accept the future without hoping to control the uncontrollable, I will be able to live now, which is the only time for living that I have.

Holding On

As I remember, recall, review, recycle, rework past experiences, I am holding on to them emotionally even though I know rationally that they are past.

I know that the past exists only in memory and in consequences. Yet in spite of the fact that the memory is only memory, I become emotionally in-

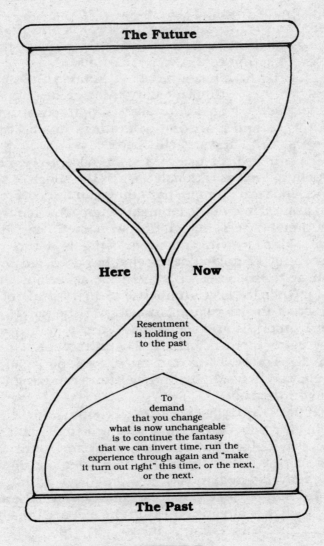

The Future

Here   Now

Resentment
is holding on
to the past

To
demand
that you change
what is now unchangeable
is to continue the fantasy
that we can invert time, run the
experience through again and "make
it turn out right" this time, or the next,
or the next.

The Past

FIGURE 7

volved with it again as though it were actuality. And instead of accepting the consequences and exploring ways of changing or utilizing them, I refuse them, and try to turn time backwards and undo them. Both acts are attempts at holding on to the past and acting as if it were still present.

More bluntly, resentment is a bulldog bite that clenches the teeth of memory into the dead past and refuses to let go. The past is slipping irretrievably away, and resenting determines to stop the universe until anger is satisfied.

Painful experiences must be accepted emotionally as well as rationally. When the shock of an experience evokes more pain than can be accepted and assimilated at the moment of impact, then the emotional processing will follow, sometimes days later. This grieving and regrieving is a way of absorbing the full impact of what has occurred and coming to believe it with the heart as well as the head. When the loss is immense, as in the death of a person or the loss of a relationship or the rejection of love, months and sometimes years of mourning may be required before the loss is accepted emotionally. The heart has a memory too, and it must be allowed to feel its pain fully before releasing its hold on the past.

When injury is an interpersonal one, the mourning takes the form of resentment which demands satisfaction from the other person. Inside the feelings of resentment there are demands, often many-layered demands.

I demand that you turn time backward and undo what is already done. (I refuse to see the obvious, that this is impossible.)

I demand that you change the unchangeable, form what is not yet formed, reform what is already formed. (I refuse to admit the obvious that this is irrational.)

I demand that you appease, pacify, grovel, suffer in atonement for your inability to do the impossible. (I refuse to accept the obvious that this is destructive to you, to me, and to our future relationship.)

"Now hold on there," I say in my resentment, "hold it right there until we get this cleared up. I'm holding out until you come across with proof, payment or penance." I'm holding on and no movement, change, growth are possible until I let go.

Holding Back

As I worry, brood, and suspect the future, I am holding back from moving freely and openly into the time that is now approaching me.

Suspicion is a fearful attempt to hold back the future. Suspecting it of the worst, I think it best to stay here, now, safe in this present moment's security and not step into the unknown.

When there has been pain between myself and another, I may be afraid to risk the possibilities of its recurring in the future, or even fear the unfolding of feelings that inevitably come when open relationship is resumed; so I hold back inside.

In my head I know that the future is not avoidable, that tomorrow cannot be managed, controlled, or determined in advance. Yet I feel those demands within me and fear blocks the open flow of experience. Again, the demands can be multiple and confused.

I demand that you control the uncontrollable and promise tomorrow, today. (I refuse to see the obvious that such promises are meaningless; you can only pledge to be all you are, if you are there then.)

I demand that you deliver the undeliverable security, shape the shapeless future events, stop the unstoppable flow of time and keep things as they are or from being what they will be. (I blind myself to the obvious that you are not God and I have no right to such god-like demands.)

If I demand the right to make you prove your trustworthiness by withholding open acceptance, or that you earn my loving regard by suffering for past slights, or pay for future closeness by agreeing to punishment or penance, I and we are holding back from both the future and the present reality of genuine relationship.

Let It Be
Forgiveness is letting what was, be gone; what will be, come; what is now, be.

In forgiving, I finish my demands on past predicaments, problems, failures and say good-by to them with finality. I cancel my predictions, suspicions, premonitions of future failure and welcome the next moment with openness to discover what will be. I make a new transaction of affirming integrity between us now.

Finishing my demands on your past acts and words requires sorting them out and making appropriate decisions. Those demands which are just can be negotiated until we reach the solution most satisfactory to us both. Those demands

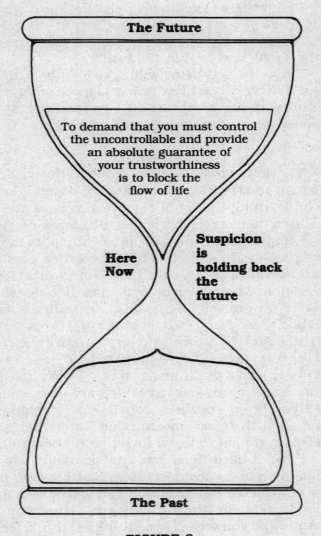

The Future

To demand that you must control
the uncontrollable and provide
an absolute guarantee of
your trustworthiness
is to block the
flow of life

Here
Now

Suspicion
is
holding back
the
future

The Past

FIGURE 8

which are pretentious, impossible and unjust can be canceled.

Forgiveness is willingly accepting the other on the basis of our loving and leveling, of our caring and confronting, agreeing to be genuine with each other here, now and in the future.

Forgiveness is being willing to let it be with the best that we can achieve now and move on into the future without repressing my own spontaneous response to you or seeking to restrict yours.

Letting Go

The ability to live cleanly between the past and its pain and the future and its fears, depends largely on learning the art of emotional release and relaxation that lets go of defenses, demands, disgust.

I find it hard, initially, to see my part in any interpersonal conflict, while the other person's part is so obvious. My own defense structure blocks my vision. When I turn my eyes inward to assess my part in the problem, a curtain of denial drops automatically so that my half of the hassle is out of sight. Instead, I see a movie—a very moving picture of the reverse emotions—projected on the screen of denial. Instead of the anger, irritableness, frustration, impatience, jealousy which are truly there, I see portrayed concern, conviction, compassion and all such "good" motivations. I must let go of defenses if I am to know myself and know you.

I find it hard to let go of my demands. My demands seem so obviously just, just because they are mine. If they are truly just they will be seen to be just in our continuing dialogue. Thus any demands that you see as I see, I think as I think, feel as I feel deserve to be canceled.

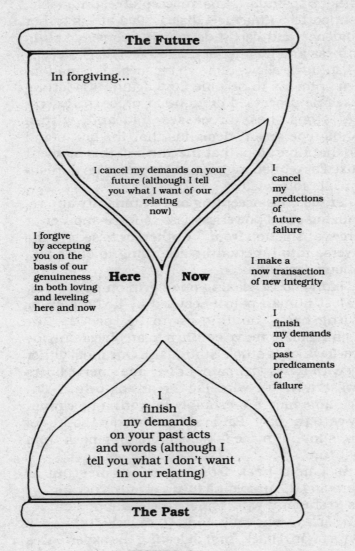

FIGURE 9

I find it hard to let go of my disgust. When another's position seems unacceptable, untenable, unsupported, I may feel disgruntled at his or her confidence and certitude which I consider stubbornness and dogmatism, and I feel disgusted.

Letting go allows one's views, feelings, emotion-laden opinions to become fluid again. It is letting oneself be processed or to be in process. Resentment stops these processes cold and, with a Joshua-type anger, demands that the sun stand still, that time stop, that the anger of this moment be fixed and unchanging until it exacts its punishment, its total victory.

Letting go is accepting one's humanity and recognizing one's powerlessness to force another or coerce satisfaction from the other, or to seduce the universe into functioning according to one's pretentious demands.

Letting go is relaxing one's grip on pain.

Most human pain is caused by holding on or holding back. Holding on to the past is like attaching one's nerve endings to an object outside oneself which is stuck, stationary. One must either stay with it to avoid pain, or feel one's nerve fibers slowly drawn into wire-like threads of torture. But since time moves inexorably forward, one cannot stay with the past. Pain results. An equal source of pain is found in the fantasy of holding back from the future.

As I hold back from entering, meeting or embracing the unfolding future, I am clenching my eyes to shut out what is nonetheless approaching.

So I may clench my stomach muscles into a ball of wire to hold back from digesting the experiences

I am taking in; or clench my cranial muscles to squeeze out the angry thoughts in a vise-like migraine that comes from choking the blood supply in arteries, veins and capillaries; or I may clench my organs to pour out stomach acid in anxiety, adrenalin in fear, sweat in lubrication for fighting or fleeing. And I feel pain!

Letting go is necessary if one is to find release from the pain. Letting go allows one to flow forward again with the movement of time, to be present once more with oneself, one's companions, one's universe.

Release from pain comes as one is willing to release the hatred being held against another.

Resentment dissipates as one gently lets go of resenting. Suspicion fades as one stops pursuing the fantasies of the other's plotting, hating or betraying. The secret is in letting go.

The attempt to "overwhelm," "fight against," or exterminate old resentments, hatreds and suspicions generally has the opposite effect. The old patterns only become more nimble and elusive. Any intensified drives to crush a part of oneself will evoke opposing forces. I change not when I am trying to be different than I am, or to be what I am not, but when I am truly and fully accepting what I am.

Saying Good-by

Saying good-by is breaking contact, breaking off conversation, breaking connection.

There is power in the act of saying good-by. It is a clear signal that one situation is finished and another is beginning. It is a decisive statement that this moment with its relationships is terminating and a new moment with a different network of relationships is here.

The inability to say good-by leaves one unable to live cleanly in the present and incapable of seeing clearly what is here, now, present before him or her. In failing to say good-by, the person carries along images of persons, after-effects of situations, dated emotions of past conflicts, obsolete perceptions that are no longer valid, fixed opinions that are not open to reconsideration, reified judgments that have turned to stone. A whole coterie of ghosts, phantoms and dramatic fantasies hover over his thinking, plaguing him with fears and danger warnings.

The refusal to say good-by is most frequently the result of being stuck between the conflicted feelings of love and hate toward another person or a past relationship. When one both loves and hates another but can only accept the loving, then saying good-by seems impossible. In some deep way a person knows that cutting off the relationship will release a hidden turmoil of feelings. The anger and disgust will come out sooner or later, one fears, so one sits on the feelings, resists bringing them to an aware ending and so evades a full confrontation with what is within.

The inability to say good-by is much like pathological grieving—when the frozen feelings cannot be mourned out because love and anger are painfully mixed; to cry out the pain would also let out the rage. Or it is like the arrested developmental process of staying stuck in a given stage of childhood because moving to the next requires one's making the learning and taking the responsibility for that stage of life and getting on into the next.

To say good-by is to feel both joy and sadness of separation. Joy that a past experience is now complete. Sadness that it cannot continue indefinitely.

To say good-by is to accept both love and hate in recollection: love for those parts of the relationship which were uniting, freeing, joyful; hate for the parts which devalued and detracted from wholeness and full selfhood.

To say good-by is to let go of the past—without rewriting its history to suit my pride system, reworking its failure through rituals of undoing, resuffering its pain in an attempt at atonement. And it is to let oneself go into the future, free, unencumbered, and relatively unafraid.

Risking Trust

Letting go, saying good-by and risking trust are sequential steps toward freedom. Venturing trust is a risk, in fact trust occurs only when there is a risk involved. When one is aware that a desired outcome is dependent upon another's behavior— and one stands to lose more than would be gained by success—yet risks the outcome into the other's hands, trust is expressed.

Life is a series of trust ventures: it is trust risked, risk rewarded, new trust ventured, and new risks taken. Living is a constant movement between the twin tensions of trust and risk. As they go hand in hand, or join hands in willing forgiveness, we grow.

Exploring the Biblical Basis

Let the past be past. Be present in this present moment. Welcome the future. Paul models such clean time boundaries in dealing with his own experience; he affirms it in responding to others.

Philippians 3:4-21—Paul's view of self:
vv. 4-7 Forgetting what lies behind—
The past has high performance
and is reason for self-confidence,
with a record worthy of real pride,
with a history of high success.
The past is forgotten.

vv. 8-10 Recognizing what is now—
The present is a time for faith,
a time for knowing and being known,
a time for sharing in joy and pain,
a time for embracing what is and can be.
The present is claimed.

vv. 12-16 Reaching out to the future—
The future is rich with promise:
it offers excitement in goals,
it promises the prize of maturity,
it calls us to the presence of God.
The future welcomes us.

Second Corinthians 5:11-21—Paul's view of others:
vv. 11-16 Forgetting what lies behind—
We no longer view persons
from a human point of view.
The old is no longer in control.

We no longer live for ourselves, v. 15.
No longer pride ourselves
in position or performance, v. 12.

vv. 17,18 Recognizing what is now—
In Christ, a new creation has come.
The old is gone, the new has come.
Now we are reconciled.
Now we are at peace (6:1,2).
Past trespasses are released.

vv. 19-21 Reaching out to the future—
The future is open before us.
We are reconciled to God,
We share in God's reconciling work,
We work together with God.

1. Collect references to the decisive acts of God in cutting us loose from the bondage of the past. Find passages which declare God has "blotted out," "buried," "sunk in the sea," "put to death," "forgotten," "erased," the impact of the past.

2. Read the book of Hosea, making notes on God's indiscourageable love, God's willingness to release us from the past, God's eagerness to embrace us now when there is a genuine turning toward Him. In forgiving, we do the same.

For Further Experience
PERSONAL
1. Experience Resentment. Sit facing into a corner with your arms crossed, hands

in tight fists, your teeth clenched, frowning, and recall a resentment from as recent past as possible. Let your feelings grow by repeating demands that the other hurt, pay, be punished, suffer, change everything. STOP. Now reflect on what has happened to you. Note the bodily feelings, the cyclical thoughts that come up so easily when one gives the self permission to brood. Now release those demands, turn your chair around and send prayers, thoughts, feelings of goodwill toward that person in loving acceptance. STOP. Reflect again on the feelings, sensations, bodily responses. Choose love.

2. Experience Suspicion. Go into a closet or some place for withdrawal. Focus thoughts on a person whose trustworthiness is important to you. Let the mistrust fill you. STOP. Reflect, experience the feelings and sensations. Be aware of what, how, when you do this to yourself. Now think thoughts of trusting, valuing, loving, praying gratefully for that person. STOP. Reassess your mental, emotional, physical responses. Choose trust.

3. Now note how resentment is holding on to the past, suspicion is holding back from the future, and choose two new ways of responding—one backward, one forward—for this week's experiment in being more free.

In Small Group

1. For self-disclosing, finish the following sentence fragments:

When I am resenting, I feel. . .

When I hold on to the past, I am stopping myself from. . .

When I hold back from the future I am scaring myself with. . .

I get something out of suspicion and I suspect that it is. . .

2. For discussion, consider: I let go of the past in response to another's repentance; I move into the future in response to another's expression of clear intentions; I reach out now in response to his or her genuineness in loving and leveling in this moment.

Which of these is most difficult?

How do I make it hard for myself?

Are they not equally important steps to take?

What can I do to learn new freedom in all three?

**Forgiveness is
renewed
repentance.**

**The real enduring issues of
justice,
integrity, and the
righteousness of
right
relationships are
resolved and
restructured into the
restored
relationships.**

**So we are free to
love,
live, and
risk again.**

4 ■ Forgive

By Renewing Repentance

"I know Larry is sorry for wrecking the car; he wants me to forgive and forget, but first I need to know if he's learned anything from the experience.

"One week ago Larry took our new Volvo to go out with his girl. Before the evening ended, he had filled the car with eight kids; they killed a case of beer and sideswiped three parked cars in testing out how a Volvo corners at 40 miles an hour at the center of the town square.

"Yes I'm willing to forgive. Yes I care about Larry. Yes he can be trusted with the Volvo again. But first I want to know that he will be more responsible in the future, that he will respect the whole family's rights to use an unwrecked car, and that he will help cover the increase in insurance costs from the wreck."

Forgiveness includes, requires, follows, repentance.

Forgiveness recognizes what has really happened, owns the hurt incurred, responds to the other person with integrity, and affirms new behavior for the future with genuine intentions.

Repentance is the central task of forgiving and being forgiven. Where there is no repentance, there is no true forgiveness. Perhaps no proposition on forgiving will evoke more immediate disagreement than the insistence that repentance is indispensable.

The virtue of loving acceptance is so deeply prized and so widely cited as the central definition of forgiveness that repentance has become separated from the act of forgiving. A frequent working definition is "forgiveness is an unconditional gift of love." Any expectation of repentance as an integral part of forgiving is seen as the imposition of conditions, or as magical thinking that time can be turned backward, or as a fantasy that what is done can be undone, or as a puritan process of inducing additional guilt, or as a judgmental tactic to exact punishment, or as a pietistic strategy for coercing moral conformity. Repentance can serve any and occasionally all of the above functions, and it can also be a transaction of integrity that works justice out of injury.

Two contrasting positions on the nature of genuine forgiving focus on the issue of repentance: the one perspective holding that forgiveness precedes repentance, which then follows as a result; the other sees repentance as the core element in effecting forgiveness.

Unconditional Forgiveness?

Position one: Forgiveness precedes repentance. "There has been no move from Alex to suggest that he has the slightest regret about what happened. No evidence that he has any change of heart. For all I know, he still explains his actions as inevitable. So should I forgive him without any further word?"

Bill puzzled over the low receipts at the prescription counter for weeks before he finally set a trap to check up on his employee's records. Then he discovered that Alex was only ringing up half of the sale and pocketing the extra. Since few people asked for their cash register receipts in the small country store, who would suspect?

Alex listened to Bill's confrontation impassively, walked out without a word, submitted his resignation by letter. After years of association, Bill is not satisfied to see their friendship cut off with no reconciliation. But his second attempt at conversation was cut off with, "There's just no way you can begin to understand my circumstances and why what I did was unavoidable."

"I could call again and affirm my forgiveness, perhaps that would open the door to his finally expressing repentance."

True forgiveness restores the other's freedom with no questions asked, no demands imposed, no repentance required, no revenge attempted. It does not expect, await, or invite repentance as a means to experiencing forgiveness. It sees true repentance as an emotion arising from the experience of forgiveness. When one knows that he has been loved, accepted, forgiven, then he is free to respond repen-

tantly. When one feels the reality of loving, acceptant forgiveness then the motivation to repent
springs up within.

But forgiveness comes first. It is the ground, the
base, the matrix out of which authentic repenting
arises. Repentance is motivated by the experience
of forgiveness, not the other way around. "No one
ever truly repents until he or she has experienced
the possibility of forgiveness," John Calvin is often
quoted as saying. Out of grace experienced emerges
repentance, restitution and restoration of relationships. This perspective tends to equate forgiveness and love.

Unconditional Love
Position two: Repentance precedes forgiveness.

"I was insensitive to your feelings yesterday
when I criticized your work so harshly. I was un-
loading a lot of other frustration about a whole
series of things that have gone wrong recently and I
put it all on you. I recognize it was unfair, I'll be
acting differently in the future."

(This is repentance. Owning what has been
done, choosing a new behavior, expressing clear
intentions for the future. It is the one step possible
in reaching out for forgiveness.)

Forgiveness is an act of integrity which recognizes that wrongdoing has occurred, has been ac-
knowledged, and has been dealt with responsibly
by both parties involved. When repentance is overlooked, ignored, bypassed, or postponed, the
appropriate response is love, not forgiveness.

Love chooses to see the other as a valued person
once more in spite of the wrongdoing. Love restores

its attitudes of prizing and caring for the other. Love is the basis for forgiveness but it is only the first step. Repentance is the second. Love restores the equal regard for the other as a person of worth. This is step one. Then follows the negotiations of trust until right relationships are once more achieved. When trust is restored, and there is mutual recognition that constructive relationships have been resumed, forgiveness has become a reality.

Is this merely a chicken and egg riddle? If both repentance and forgiveness are needed to renegotiate relationships with integrity and openness, what does it matter which one comes first as long as both do occur?

Jesus' words are clear and precise on this issue: "Keep watch on yourselves. If your brother wrongs you, rebuke him; and if he repents, forgive him. Even if he wrongs you seven times in a day and comes back to you seven times saying 'I'm sorry,' you are to forgive him" (Luke 17:3,4, *NEB*).

Note the sequence of events: (1) There is a situation of wrongdoing, (2) in which the wrongdoer is still perceived as a brother (3) who is to be confronted. (4) If he then repents, (5) forgive him (6) without holding past failures against him (7) even when there is sevenfold evidence that the other's repentance has not resulted in perfection (8) and there is a repetition of the offense (9) and there will be a willing attitude to see the other's repentance as genuine on the basis of honesty expressed in covenanting now. Pain. Renewed love. Confrontation. Repentance. Forgiveness. In this order, if it is to achieve this effect.

Not Penance, Repentance

A word of clarification, definition and negation are appropriate when "repentance" is discussed.

First negation: Repentance is not penance. It is not a process of earning acceptance by groveling, by putting oneself down first so no one else has to do it for you. Nor is it a process of grieving in making oneself unhappy for a sufficient length of time until one deserves to be happy again.

Then clarification: Repentance is not remorse. Regret and remorse are profound emotions and they may be appropriate to the experience of repentance, but they are not one and the same. One may mourn for opportunities lost and values negated, but such mourning arises out of sadness for what was and was not, not out of strategies for paying one's way with pain to get back into right relationships. Remorse is a process of shaming, of self-destruction by means of lowered self-esteem.

After writing a straightforward confrontation to the Christians at Corinth, who were overlooking an incestuous relationship within the congregation, the apostle Paul writes a second time in a way which clarifies the distinction between remorse and repentance:

"Even if I did wound you by the letter I sent, I do not now regret it. I may have been sorry for it when I saw that the letter had caused you pain, even if only for a time; but now I am happy, not that your feelings were wounded but that the wound led to a change of heart. You bore the smart as God would have you bear it, and so you are no losers by what we did. For the wound which is borne in God's way brings a change of heart too salutary to regret; but

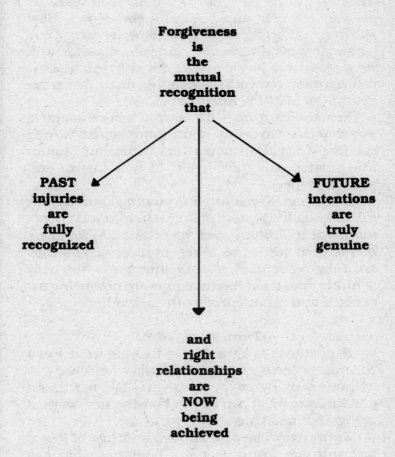

**Forgiveness
is
the
mutual
recognition
that**

**PAST
injuries
are
fully
recognized**

**FUTURE
intentions
are
truly
genuine**

**and
right
relationships
are
NOW
being
achieved**

FIGURE 10

the hurt which is borne in the world's way brings death. You bore your hurt in God's way, and see what its results have been! It made you take the matter seriously and vindicate yourselves. How angered you were, how apprehensive! How your longing for me awoke, yes, and your devotion and your eagerness to see justice done! At every point you have cleared yourselves of blame in this trouble" (2 Cor. 7:8-11, *NEB*).

Remorse is a hurt borne in a self-destructive way that leads to death. Repentance is pain turned creative, hurt that moves toward healing, injury that invites us to live again in new justice and mutual respect.

Definition: *Repentance is owning what was in full acknowledgement of the past, and it is choosing what will be in open responsibility for one's behavior in the future.* In repentance, past injuries are fully recognized, future intentions are truly genuine, and right relationships are now being expressed and experienced with each other.

Turn, Turn, Turn

Repentance is a turning, a turning from and a turning to. In repenting, one turns from what was without denying or ignoring what has been; and one turns to what can be by choosing new ways of being and behaving.

Turn from: The past is past. To let go of it and face into the future is not a denial of what has happened, it is the full recognition that it has taken place and that its place is in the past. Since it is history it cannot be changed. It is no longer available except in recall. It can be accepted or owned;

celebrated or regretted. It cannot be evaded or avoided without blocking growth. Change comes as one owns the past as one's own. I change, not when I am attempting to be what I am not, but when I am owning what, where, who I truly am. Then I am free to turn from, to change from, to grow.

Turn to: Having owned my past behavior with both its failures and successes, I am free to choose new alternatives for the future. Where I have not kept faith, I can choose fidelity. Where I have not told, done, or been the truth to another, I can choose renewed integrity. Life is a continuous series of turnings, from, to and with.

Forego, Forget, Forgive

When forgiveness foregoes repentance, don't trust it.

When forgiveness forgets the real enduring unresolved issues of justice, integrity and the righteousness of right relationships, don't believe it.

When forgiveness takes justice, integrity and right relationships seriously, risk it.

Forego: Real reconciliation is hopeless; the best we can do is to tolerate the differences between us without stirring up the pain of the past. Real negotiations are helpless to change what has taken place or to alter what will take place again. The most we can do is to make do with what we have. So forego any expectations of working through repentance and reconstruction of the relationship.

Forget: Real reconciliation is painful. Someone always gets hurt. The personal implications of any and all differences simply cannot be ignored. It's best for one party to absorb the hurt and forget the demands of justice. Real negotiations are impossible without reaching an impasse. The better choice is to forget any inclination to seek repentance and recreate the relationship.

Forgive: Real reconciliation is possible if one is willing to trust. Real negotiations are possible if one is willing to risk. The willingness to turn from mistrust and trust again, the willingness to venture out from safe withdrawal and risk again are two parts of genuine repentance. Both steps invite repenting and rebuilding of the relationship in return.

Care enough to trust again.

Care enough to risk again.

Care enough to turn and invite change in return.

Care enough to not forgive until repentance is genuine.

___

Exploring the Biblical Basis

The integral relationship of repentance and forgiveness is central in the teaching of Jesus. "Repent, for the kingdom of heaven is at hand," are His opening words (Matt. 4:17, *RSV*; see Mark 1:15). Examine again His succinct statements on response to the brother or sister:

Scripture	*Your Notes*
Take heed to yourselves;	
If your brother sins,	
rebuke him,	
and if he repents,	
forgive him;	

FOREGO Repenting	FORGIVE in mutual Repentance	FORGET Repentance
Accept the other no questions asked. It's not important.	Face the pain own the injury work with feelings affirm intentions	Ignore the hurt smile, accept be nice
Pessimism Resentment	Patience Persistence	Passivity Denial
Turn Off the other	Turn From past pain	Turn In on self
	Turn to a forgiven future	

FIGURE 11

and if he sins against you
seven times in the day,
and turns to you seven times
and says, "I repent,"
you must forgive him
(Luke 17:3,4, *RSV*).

1. Our understanding of forgiveness man-to-man, woman-to-woman must parallel our insight into forgiveness God-to-man/woman. (1) Grace affirms love, so forgiveness is offered. (2) Repentance turns toward that love, so forgiveness is accepted. (3) Reconciliation occurs, so forgiveness is experienced. Compare Acts 2:38-41.

2. Our task in claiming forgiveness is the open confession and authentic repentance that receives forgiving love. Read 1 John 1:5-10. Note that the response of open owning is what invites the faithfulness of the forgiver and invokes justice in the forgiveness. Now note how this is paralleled in John's teaching about brother-to-brother relationships, 1 John 2:9-11; 3:11-18; 4:7-21.

For Further Experience

PERSONAL

1. I believe that repentance results from forgiveness. (Write a brief argument pro or con.)
2. I believe that repentance precedes forgiveness. (Write a brief statement yes or no.)
3. Now reflect on your own experiences of forgiveness. Which came first for you? Which opened the door to deeper reconciliation? How has your experience influenced the statements you made above?

IN SMALL GOUP

1. Discuss the differences between repentance and remorse. Contrast Peter's experience of repentance, and Judas's paralysis in remorse. Reflect on which you have felt, expressed, experienced and with what effect?

2. Describe your own impulses to do penance, to grovel a bit to earn acceptance, to give a gift of material, of kindness, of being nice to try to undo or redo the situation. Note how one of these—or another strategy—seems preferable to open repenting.

3. Trace a history of your feelings about the word *repentance.* Is it a bad word? A good word? A bad word just now becoming good? A punitive word? A hopeful word?

4. Discuss how sincere repentance is the only proper request for forgiveness. (I will not ask another for forgiveness. There are no biblical models for such in the New Testament. My part is confession and affirmation of repentance. If the other perceives this is genuine, forgiveness is given and received as a gift. If I ask for it, it is experienced as blackmail since to refuse, postpone, or to say "I'm not ready yet," is to appear to be "unforgiving." Thus the Bible reports that unforgiving is unforgivable. Thus I confess/repent. I receive the assurance as a gift of grace.)

In a world of
   flawed
   communication,
community is possible
   through
   understanding
   others.

In a world of
   painful
   alienation,
community is created by
   accepting
   others.

In a world of
   broken
   trust,
community is sustained by
   forgiveness.

5 ■ Forgive

By Rediscovering Community

"If he shows his face in this community again, he's asking for trouble. And there are a lot of people who would be more than happy to give it to him."

This normally coolheaded businessman is commenting with emotion on the youth pastor in their church who, during the tense sixties, took a strong counterculture position against the Viet Nam war, against the expensive standard of living of the wealthy families, against the political views of the majority, and widened the existing gaps between youth and their parents until the community was torn apart by its inability to live with such internal tensions.

"We lost half-a-dozen young people from our families who left and have never come back. It was

largely, not all of course, but to a large extent, his
fault. When he left no one said good-by. No one who
remained shed a tear. But so many of our kids lost
faith in everything, and that has caused a lot of
sorrow. He did us an awful lot of harm and there's
no way to undo it; there's no forgiveness for destroying families."

(Forgiveness is the essential substance of community. When it is shattered, the central nervous
system that sustains the community is blocked or
cut.)

The Estranged Community
"Once upon a time we were a close community,
then came 'X,' bringing distance, mistrust, and
estrangement, or 'Y' bringing fear, suspicion and
silent withdrawal, or 'Z' causing all this anger and
resentment of each other. It's all his or her fault. If
we could put it all at his doorstep, or make her
suffer deeply enough to pay for it, perhaps things
could be better."

This myth has been told, retold, written, rewritten for centuries. When an explanation is needed
for the pain of an alienated community, the myth of
a scapegoat is an ever available answer. And it is so
frequently needed. Any community is only a year
away from estrangement. All that is needed is for
forgiveness to end, for acceptance to break down,
for trust to turn to mistrust and understanding
ceases.

Seldom, if ever, is this the fault of one person
alone. It takes at least two persons to have a problem to begin with, and generally it requires a whole
community's complicity, whether passive or active,

I
am
I am I
I am one
I am many
I am a community
of persons known, loved, hated.
Within me lives a collection of people
I have followed or fought, accepted or avoided,
chosen as good models, rejected as bad models,
prized, valued, idealized and/or disliked, devalued, despised.
They are all there, remembered or forgotten somewhere within.
I have learned from all of them, willingly or not.
I have grown from their gifts, good or bad.
I have gained much because they were there.
They are my teachers, my guides.
They make up my museum
my inner community
my community
of the spirit.
Because of
them all
I am
I

FIGURE 12

to produce a real climate of estrangement. People join in withholding understanding, or neglect trying to reach new understandings when differences arise. Then a finger of blame is pointed and suspicion rises and conversations between fearful parties become superficial and then cease all together. If nature abhors a vacuum, a community finds it even more abhorrent; and the silence is quickly filled with rumors, with negative valuations of each other, with criticisms and closed judgments.

Forgiveness, the final form love must take in creating a healing community, has disappeared, and the hope of rebuilding it grows ever dimmer.

The Forgiving Community

Forgiveness springs from the healing context of community. It is possible not because of the benevolent superiority of the forgiver, but because of the choice to be transparent to the forgiving possibility that is present in the community that supports, sustains, stimulates one even in the midst of tragedy.

Forgiveness, as an emotion or action, emerges from the depth experiences of love that have made up your and my inner community of spirit (the past relationships of love and acceptance that have occurred not only in our life cycle but in the thousands of years of divine-human experience which precede this moment of decision), and from the rich experiences of love that are called out by the present communities that enable us to be human. (Even the isolated prisoner has both an inner community of the past and a chosen community of present allegiance with whom he or she is affiliated in the spirit.)

The Supportive Community

When you and I join in creating community, we take up the work of initiating, achieving and celebrating forgiveness; for it is forgiving that allows us to turn our injuries into new commitments, our tragic failures into new covenants. A major task is creating a supportive climate in which the willingness to forgive is constantly nurtured and rewarded. This "willingness" is the voluntary intention to work through to restored relationships. Such willingness does not occur independently of the significant others who make up our life support system. We call our compassion, concern and caring from each other.

The climate which nurtures such supportive relationships has three constant qualities which are givens, and three situational qualities which are guarantees. The givens are there as a stable basis for nurturing trust, warmth, confidence, and the willingness to reconcile. The guarantees are available when relationships break down, when trust erodes, when communication stalls and forgiveness and reconciliation are needed. The givens are *availability, authenticity* and *acceptance.* The guarantees are *recognition, reinforcement* and *rewards.*

Given: Availability. Friendship in community is mutual availability. The degree of reciprocal availability between persons defines the strength of their relationship. In a deeply committed relationship, there are few conditions on availability.

In a casual relationship, one is available on a very limited basis. To be physically, emotionally and spiritually available to another, at the level appropriate to the relationship being experienced, invites trust.

A covenant of availability undergirds community. When presence is a given, one need not fear the withdrawal of significant people when things go wrong. Their presence is an unquestioned certainty which reassures the community member—consciously and unconsciously—that others will be there for him or her in any time of stress or distress.

In giving presence to another I am saying, "I am available, I am truly for you, I am present here with you now in success or failure, in high performance or low, in items of being "right" or times of feeling "wrong.""

Given: Authenticity. Genuineness in the forgiving community grows from the shared authenticity of people who feel safe to express their real selves and increasing levels of their whole selves to each other. In being our authentic selves with others, we are free to set limits, free to affirm values, free to assert wants, free to confront with differences, free to express caring. All these strengthen the ties that knit us into community.

A covenant of authenticity liberates a community to be truly forgiving. When genuineness is given, both poles of experience are called out. Both caring and confronting can occur, both anger and appreciation, both contrasting values and concern for relationships.

In giving genuineness to another I am pledging: "I stand with you. Nothing in you is foreign to me.

GUARANTEES:
The
response
of
healing
community

1. Recognition
2. Reinforcement
3. Reward

Support for doing, for performance

GIVENS: The foundation of community

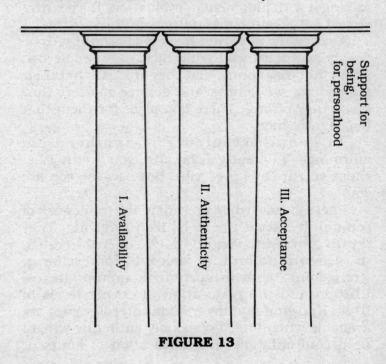

Support for being, for personhood

I. Availability

II. Authenticity

III. Acceptance

FIGURE 13

We share both the wisdom and folly of being human. We feel both the joy and the pain of life's situations. We can risk being real throughout it all, together."

Given: Acceptance. Caring about another, caring for another, expressing caring to another are all dimensions of solidarity within the forgiving community. To care about another is to be aware of another's pain, anger or frustration. To care for another is to offer support, understanding and appropriate help as it is needed. To express caring to another is to put affection and appreciation into words as well as acts. As caring is offered without mixing it with judgment or evaluation, the positive regard felt is without conditions.

A covenant of caring frees a community to be deeply acceptant and truly inclusive. People can sense that they count, that they are "in," that their happiness, wholeness and service matter; they know they belong: There is a place for them that has significance.

In giving acceptance to another I am affirming—"I accept you because you are; not because you are as I prescribe, but because you are you."

These givens, when present in the framework of community, set it free to be truly forgiving. They are the antecedent conditions that open the system to recognize failure, to welcome confession of wrongdoing, to invite repentance, appropriate restitution and the restoration of deeper levels of trust. Knowing that my friends and colleagues are available when I need response, authentic when I need confrontation and clarification of limits or

GUARANTEES:
The
response
to
problems
situations
conflicts
as
they
arise
within
community

1. RECOGNITION:
I recognize your hurt/being hurtful and your responsible handling of the pain;

2. REINFORCEMENT:
I support your choice to work through the conflict responsibly.

3. REWARDS:
I value/respect/appreciate/am grateful for your rebuilding relationship.

GIVENS: The foundation of community: **GIVENS**

I. Availability
I am available, I am truly for you, I am present here and now.

II. Authenticity
I am with you as a whole person with both caring and confronting.

III. Acceptance
I accept you as you are, simply because, and only because, you are you.

FIGURE 14

boundaries, and acceptant of me as a person when my behavior is approved or disapproved assures me of my place in relationship, my position as a valued member of the circle of caring humans.

Availability, authenticity and acceptance provide a context of caring which enables persons to give and receive confrontation. It provides the stability of support which allows us to offer and accept criticism. It creates a base of empathy and understanding upon which evaluating and advising can be built. It firms up an emotional floor of affirmation which then undergirds any assertiveness. It assures us of the constancy of love which invites us to level with each other.

Guaranteed: Recognition. We are created in such a way that we require regular mutual recognition from significant others. The need for recognition increases in times of stress. It is then that being avoided, ignored or passed by hurts most deeply. The forgiving community guarantees recognition of visible hurts, recognition of the person when he or she reports private and less visible injuries to personhood or self-esteem.

The temptation to practice denial when differences become painful is the ever-present curse of community. The idea that withholding recognition will help the problem go away or aid in dissipating tension, or that time heals all things, only serve to nudge us toward more and more use of denial.

Recognition is due to the persons who stand on either and both sides of an altercation: to the offender in the process of making right a wronged person; to the offended in the experience of regaining closeness and wholeness.

Recognition of another within community affirms both separateness and connectedness; that we are distinct from each other and yet alike; that we can identify with each other and yet can see the other as a unique person of dignity and integrity. In times of distress, recognition respects the other's right to work through his or her conflict independently while standing alongside with clear awareness and open feedback on what is taking place.

Recognition affirms, "I see that you are hurting (whether offender or offended). I respect your right to take the appropriate steps to resolve the issue. I reaffirm my concern for you both. I am on call, if you need me, I'm here."

Guaranteed: Reinforcement. When an injury divides persons, recognition of what has happened, now is, and still can be is the first guarantee. But it is rarely enough. The forgiving community offers reinforcement of each positive step toward reconciliation. Even when the reality of the hurt is clearly seen, owned, and admitted verbally, the great temptation is to settle for an easy solution. A simple apology without working through, an exchange of "forgiveness-words" without achieving justice, a mutual agreement to forgive and forget without reaching a new level of understanding—any of these answers are too easy. Those who stop along the way to reconciliation need a forgiving community to offer reinforcements at any stress point enroute where the tendency to call it quits becomes too great.

Reinforcements must be as varied as the situations are complex.

For those who are hesitant to look at the feelings

that exist within themselves or in another, the forgiving community can reinforce openness and self-disclosing by making it safe to feel, to own feelings, to express feelings, to negotiate feelings clearly.

For those who fear to look at problems as mutual, as two-person phenomena rather than one-way one-person predicaments, the forgiving community can reinforce candid admission that both sides have some ratio of responsibility for the occurrence of the conflict and for its resolution.

For those who hesitate to stay with a situation until justice is seen to be done by both, until there is mutual recognition that intentions are genuine on both sides, the forgiving community can reinforce following through, all the way to genuine gratitude and joint appreciation of each other.

For those who hold back from genuine repentance, the forgiving community can model, teach, practice and reinforce an ongoing repentance process that invites persons to work out repentance with a real concern for turning the negative attitudes and actions of the past toward a positive and faithful future.

Guaranteed: Rewards. "I'm glad that's over. I hope it never happens again. I've learned my lesson. I'll stay on the straight and narrow from now on." (What's going on in these words? The speaker is searching for some insight, some learning as a reward for the pain experienced.)

When no lasting rewards are given and received out of a resolution of a difference, it is not likely to produce lasting changes in behavior. The final emotions attached to the experience will tend to be mixed and often predominately negative. Shame, embarrassment, feelings of withdrawal and avoidance can all remain as a residue after the issues are all negotiated. The forgiving community offers rewards that finish the unfinished situation so that the remaining negative emotions can be recalled as positive.

The forgiving community offers respect for persons as they experience each stage of the process from awareness of pain to the celebration of renewed relationship.

The forgiving community offers appreciation for the doing of reconciling work, knowing that this is the central work of maintaining life together.

The Cost of Community

Creating, sustaining, celebrating community is costly. It requires the sacrifice of safe denial and of the civilizing force of avoidance. In community, persons are included—not ignored; invited to explore relationships—not overlooked and evaded when they provoke tensions or exaggerate uncomfortable differences.

The cost of community is in caring enough.

Caring enough to forgive.

Caring enough to refuse false "forgiveness."

Caring enough to work through repentance for past pain, recognition of the present realities, and reconstruction of our commitment for the future.

Caring enough to truly, fully forgive.

Exploring the Biblical Basis

Within community, we express an indiscourageable redemptive attitude toward wrongdoing

and wrongdoers. Of the many teaching passages
and the teachers' practices recorded in the New
Testament, the following are particularly appropriate to the focus of this chapter on living as a forgiving community.

Galatians 6:1 (RSV)
Brethren [and sisters],
if a man is overtaken
in any trespass, you
who are spiritual
should restore him in
a spirit of gentleness.
Look to yourself, lest
you too be tempted.

The focus of concern
in any scene of
wrongdoing is
restoration, recovery,
renewal of
relationships in
mutual concern for
the growth, maturity
and spiritual health of
all.

*Matthew 5:23,24
(RSV)*
So if you are offering
your gift at the altar,
and there remember
that your brother has
something against
you, leave your gift
there before the altar
and go; first to be
reconciled to your
brother, and then
come and offer your
gift.

Before any act of
piety, before any
ritual of praise, before
any meaningful
worship comes
reconciliation and
right relationships in
renewed community.
For "If I am not in
loving relationships
with the brother
whom I can see, how
can I worship rightly
the Great Lover whom
I cannot see." (Comp.
1 John 4:19-21.)

*Matthew 18:15-20
(RSV)*
If your brother sins against you, go and tell him his fault, between you and him alone. If he listens to you, you have gained your brother. But if he does not listen, take one or two others along with you, that every word may be confirmed by the evidence of two or three witnesses. If he refuses to listen to them, tell it to the church; and if he refuses to listen even to the church, let him be to you as a Gentile and a tax collector.

Note the clarity of the process:
(1) With any complaint, go immediately, directly, personally to the other. No gossiping. No indirect communication. No going public with private data. No use of others to coerce.

(2) If refused, rejected, or if reconciliation is frustrated, take one or two to witness, to assist, to clarify so that honesty, justice, fairness are done.

(3) If relationships are not yet restored, open the issue to the church. Then community can surround, support, and love the one who has broken trust even as they can love the one who is outside (Gentile) or self-alienated (tax-collector).

Truly, I say to you, whatever you bind on earth shall be bound in heaven, and whatever you loose on earth shall be loosed in heaven. Again I say to you, if two of you agree on earth about anything they ask, it will be done for them by my Father in heaven. For where two or three are gathered in my name, there am I in the midst of them.

(4) For the decisions of the community are binding, are lasting, are the expression of God's presence in the body of believers, for God is truly present in the midst of the forgiving, reconciling, discerning circle (see v. 20). (Comp. John 20:19-23.)

1. The goal is regaining the sister or brother.

2. The process is to be the body of the loving, forgiving, reconciling, community-creating Christ to each other.

3. There will be pain, there must be healing. This is the life-renewing work of living together in the Body of Christ.

For Further Experience
PERSONAL

1. Select which "given" is most important, valued, meaningful to you in community.
   _____ Availability: others are there when needed
   _____ Authenticity: others are real when met
   _____ Acceptance: others care when I'm hurting

2. Note which of the above is most weak or is miss-

ing in your present experience of community.
What can you do to initiate it or strengthen it?
Plan one specific step.
3. Check which situational response has been
most helpful to you as a community guarantee
(or is most desired if not present now).
_____ Recognition: see that I am hurting
_____ Reinforcement: respect my steps, support
me
_____ Rewards: celebrate each success, though
small.
4. Focus on one person in your community who
needs recognition, reinforcement of the steps
being taken, rewards for any venture made. Schedule time, rehearse words to offer the above.

In Small Group

1. Reexamine your group contract to explore how
you are/are not being an expression of forgiving
community to each other. A group is as healthy
as its contract is clear. Can you call it into clearer focus?
2. Review your community's covenant, whether it
is conscious, clearly expressed and voluntarily
affirmed OR if it is unconscious, unarticulated,
unnegotiated, and not fully understood by
others. A community is as healing as its covenant is clear. Can you call it into clearer understanding?
3. Report your wishes for greater community expression of the healing "givens"— availability,
authenticity, acceptance. Covenant with each
other to reach out with these to others in pain or
not yet in pain.

4. Reflect on how you exercise the three guaran-
    tees in response to human pain. Give each other
    a gift of affirmation for when and where it has
    happened in this circle or in the wider commun-
    ity. Share your renewed intentions to be a more
    responsive member of the Body of Christ.

Epilogue

On the Other Hand

With the awareness that our motives are always mixed, our thoughts are often conflicted, our emotions are usually ambivalent . . .

yet we forgive, and forgive, and forgive again . . .

and in return, we repent and turn and turn.

Forgiveness true, sometimes mixed with forgiveness false, is the human forgiveness we have to give. Humbled by its own weakness it is often the best response we can offer to the pain, the trauma, the suffering of existence.

So as we seek to be more faithful to each other, to ourselves, to God who is constantly calling us back into communion and community, let us be constantly learning more of forgiving and being forgiven.

Since nothing we strive for is ever completed, perfected, or fully realized in our lifetime, we are saved by hope.

Since nothing we covenant is ever fulfilled, kept, held in trust in every sense in our life together, we are saved by love.

Since nothing we intend is ever faultless, and nothing we attempt ever without error, and nothing we achieve without some measure of that finitude and fallibility we call humanness, we are saved by forgiveness.

So let us forgive, for in forgiving, we too are forgiven.

Most areas of truth are too great to be dealt with from only one perspective. There are two sides to every great concern. To look again at the issue of forgiveness, turn to the other side of this book.

So let us forgive as gently and genuinely as is possible in any situation of conflict between us.

So let us forgive as fully and as completely as we are able in the circumstances of our misunderstandings.

So let us reach out for reconciliation as openly and authentically as possible for the levels of maturity we have each achieved.

So let us forgive freely, fully, at times even foolishly, but with all the integrity that is within us.